Praise for *Patience* by Allan Lokos

"*Patience* is an exquisite gift, a healing sanctuary, a balm for the soul. Allan Lokos gently guides us through the dark wood of the frantic, fearful reactivity that grows and festers in our too-hurried lives, negotiating safe passage through a world gone mad with impossible speed and inhuman expectations. He invites us to explore the root causes of our own impatience, offering simple tools of mindfulness, curiosity, and merciful attention as reliable practices for cultivating contentment, ease, and genuine peace within ourselves, our relationships, and the very real world. Make no mistake—Allan is no Pollyanna. He bravely lifts up the undeniably fierce, ugly consequences of our anger, violence, and impatient harming of ourselves and others, while confidently promising that these characteristics—too conveniently dismissed as "human nature"—can in fact be skillfully transformed into authentic strength, wisdom, courage, and inspiring leadership. Allan Lokos has offered us a precious jewel, a path to freedom, a fragrance of grace, for which we may all feel deeply and humbly grateful."

—Wayne Muller, author of *Legacy of the Heart* and *A Life of Being, Having, and Doing Enough*

"Allan Lokos has written an essential and profound book that can change your life. Spiritual growth is not like fast food. It takes time for its roots to grow, and that requires us to be receptive and patient. *Patience* delves into its vital subject with wisdom and compassion and offers us a path to our own higher self. Understanding the challenges of our hurried and harried world, Lokos has written a remarkable and practical guide to becoming a truly patient and spiritually effective person."

—Rabbi Zalman Schachter-Shalomi, author of *Jewish with Feeling* and *All Breathing Life Adores Your Name*

"This book, both practical and profound, is a wonderful demonstration of just how to bring patience and a new way of being right into our daily lives. It is filled with insight, warmth, and compassion."

—Sharon Salzberg, author of *Real Happiness* and *Lovingkindness*

"Drawing on Buddhist teachings and his own deep wisdom, Allan Lokos reminds us of the peace and freedom that are possible when we cultivate genuine patience. The stories and exercises give practical guidance in coming home to an openhearted presence in the midst of difficulty. This book is a compelling and beautiful invitation to pause and arrive fully in our life."

—Tara Brach, Ph.D., author of *Radical Acceptance*

"In this gem of a book Allan Lokos invites us to attend to and practice what is perhaps the most overlooked of all spiritual qualities. *Patience* is an important read for everyone."

—Andrew Olendzki, Ph.D., Senior Scholar, Barre Center for Buddhist Studies, author of *Unlimiting Mind*

"Allan Lokos has a depth of experience that is woven throughout this fine book. He reaches with both mind and heart into the nature of patience. As Lewis and Clark mapped our way into the timeless beauty of the Northwest, Lokos is a very wise and human guide who breaks trail into the country of patience, marking all the sacred sites along the way and honoring all the sacred guides who have come before."

—Mark Nepo, author of *The Book of Awakening* and *As Far as the Heart Can See*

"Down-to-earth, full of ways to become more patient in challenging situations at home and at work, this book helps you develop one of the most important of all virtues for fast-paced, stressful, and often frustrating life today."

—Rick Hanson, Ph.D., author of *Buddha's Brain: The Practical Neuroscience of Happiness, Love, and Wisdom*

Patience

Patience

THE ART OF PEACEFUL LIVING

Allan Lokos

JEREMY P. TARCHER/PENGUIN
a member of Penguin Group (USA) Inc.
New York

JEREMY P. TARCHER/PENGUIN
Published by the Penguin Group
Penguin Group (USA) Inc., 375 Hudson Street, New York,
New York 10014, USA • Penguin Group (Canada), 90 Eglinton Avenue East,
Suite 700, Toronto, Ontario M4P 2Y3, Canada (a division of Pearson Penguin Canada Inc.) •
Penguin Books Ltd, 80 Strand, London WC2R 0RL, England • Penguin Ireland,
25 St Stephen's Green, Dublin 2, Ireland (a division of Penguin Books Ltd) •
Penguin Group (Australia), 250 Camberwell Road, Camberwell, Victoria 3124, Australia (a division of
Pearson Australia Group Pty Ltd) • Penguin Books India Pvt Ltd, 11 Community Centre,
Panchsheel Park, New Delhi–110 017, India • Penguin Group (NZ), 67 Apollo Drive,
Rosedale, North Shore 0632, New Zealand (a division of Pearson New Zealand Ltd) •
Penguin Books (South Africa) (Pty) Ltd, 24 Sturdee Avenue,
Rosebank, Johannesburg 2196, South Africa

Penguin Books Ltd, Registered Offices: 80 Strand, London WC2R 0RL, England

Published simultaneously in Canada

Grateful acknowledgment is made for permission to reprint previously published material:

"Do not be troubled, God, though they say 'mine'" by Rainer Maria Rilke, translated by Babette Deutsch, from *Poems from the Book of Hours*, copyright ©1941 by New Directions Publishing Corporation. Reprinted by permission of New Directions Publishing Corp.

ISBN 978-1-58542-900-4

Printed in the United States of America
1 3 5 7 9 10 8 6 4 2

Book design by Meighan Cavanaugh

To my many teachers,

both those I sought

and those who found me,

those on two legs and those on four,

those with feathers and those with fins;

you have been so patient.

This inquiry does not seek theoretical knowledge,
for we are inquiring not to understand virtue, but to become virtuous,
otherwise our inquiry shall have been of little use;
we look to examine the nature of actions, specifically how we are to do them,
for this determines the very nature of character that evolves.

—Aristotle

CONTENTS

Introduction 1

Starting Patiently 17

Patience with Self 39

The Body 57

Impermanence 60

Unsatisfactoriness 62

Not-Self 65

Profile in Patience: Michael Naranjo 68

Relationships 81

Intimacy 82

Children 95

The Words We Speak 104

Profile in Patience: Lisa 113

At the Watercooler 123

Technology 134

Profile in Patience: Noël Carmichael 142

What Would a Sage Do? 149

Profile in Patience: Venerable Metteyya 172

Bodhi Shakyadita 179

The Art of Peaceful Living 185

Mindfulness 186

Insight 194

Patience as a Way of Life 199

Acknowledgments 207

Appendix A: "I feel . . ." Words 209

Appendix B: Stressors That Can Lead to Impatience 215

Suggested Reading 217

Patience

INTRODUCTION

It is said that the next teacher we need will surely appear. Our job is to be ready. Some traditions suggest that, when needed, the teacher can be a ferocious warrior. She wields a mighty sword as she faces the powerful inner forces of our ego and conditioned thinking. Often it takes a dramatic event for the teacher to be heard, a crisis perhaps stemming from a serious accident, a life-threatening illness, the loss of a loved one, or an addiction that lands one in the gutter.

Most of us meet more than one of these teachers on our life's journey. We tend to resist them at first, but then, with courage and resolve, we do battle and ultimately forge some degree of victory. We accumulate particles of wisdom along the way as we traverse gracefully onward toward the finish line. The warrior image is often suggested because insights and clarity are frequently gained only through strenuous inner battles. Imagine then my surprise and delight when a great opening of consciousness suddenly revealed itself one evening with no drama, no angst, and no turmoil.

It was, in fact, as peaceful a summer evening as one could imagine, gently embodying the soothing grace of the idyllic music that was playing in the background. My dear friend and I were reflecting casually about this and that as we often do after dinner, when suddenly I sat up straight and asked her to repeat what she had just said. "Just about every mistake I have ever made and every unkind word I have ever spoken might have been avoided if I had been more patient," she said again, speaking more slowly than she had before. I thought it was a stunning statement revealing remarkable insight. As I thought more about it I realized that the same was likely true for me. The discomfort, stress, and suffering I had experienced and caused others to experience from time to time throughout my life would have been dramatically reduced, if not completely avoided, had I understood and practiced greater patience. It also seemed to me that what was true for the two of us was likely true for the vast majority of sentient beings on this planet.

Buddhists believe that all phenomena arise from causes and conditions. This book, or your e-reader, didn't just appear in your hands. Specific past actions brought about this unique moment as is the case with every moment. This is called *dependent origination* or, simply, *contingencies*. One contingent factor in the publishing of a book would obviously be someone's decision to write it. In the case of this volume I remember the occasion well, the moment of propagation that was the birth of this book. I recall it being just after nine that summer evening when I excused myself for a moment, dashed to the computer, and jotted down my first note: "Just about every mistake I have ever made and every unkind word I have ever spoken might have been avoided if I had been more patient." It took patience for me not to disappear for the rest of the evening so I could continue writing.

I have not always been so clear as to when or if I made the decision that got me deeply involved in a project, a relationship, or even a career. I don't mean that I have wandered through life in a hazy somnambulistic state; at least I hope that is not the case. Impulse, going with what was, rather than patient consideration of pertinent information, was the style of my early days. Therefore, from time to time, I wouldn't know when or if I had made the initiatory decision that led me to where I was in life at a particular moment. As an example, although it was many years ago, I clearly remember my first big audition and being cast in the original Broadway company of *Oliver!* However, what I can't remember is ever making the major decision that preceded it. Specifically, when did I actually decide to pursue a career as a professional singer? Perhaps some of the most significant events in our lives are simply born of causes and conditions, contingent factors that come together with or without our conscious choice. Phenomena arise and we find ourselves guiding an already rolling chariot along a path of (we hope) joy and good fortune.

Being a pragmatic sort, not comfortable with dogma and "incontrovertible" doctrine, I've chosen to offer herein more than theory and philosophy. *Patience: The Art of Peaceful Living* accompanies the reader through the ups and downs of everyday life, and forges, through practical methodologies, a path to becoming a calmer, happier, more patient presence within oneself, in relationships, in the workplace, and in the world.

The development of genuine, open-minded patience may very well lead one to also examine one's experience of anger and its root causes. Although impatience and anger are not the same, they live in the same neighborhood. In fact, it is as if they live in the same house with barely a flimsy curtain between them, anger ready to join in when impatience shows the slightest interest in emerging from its thin-shelled cocoon. Not coincidentally, the journey that develops patience is traveled along a path similar to that which undermines the deceiving appeal of anger and what at times can appear to be anger's uncontrollable nature. I say *deceiving appeal* because we can experience a certain rush of hormonal satisfaction with an outpouring of draconian fury. However, as many of us know, the damage caused to ourselves and others by such outbursts can be devastating. Likewise, an ongoing suppression of angry thoughts and feelings can lead to serious psychological consequences. Regrettably, many women in our society have been raised to believe that they must not give expression to "negative" feelings, impatience and anger being primary on the list. Although the negative potential of impatience is great, suppression of feelings is also laden with peril. Expressing feelings, from mild irritability to wrathful indignation, in a manner that is skillful and beneficial requires wisdom coupled with compassion for ourselves and those around us.

Remaining calm and in a state of equanimity, yet vibrant and engaged in the face of life's constantly changing nature, is one of the great ongoing challenges faced by sentient beings. Not being emotionally and mentally shredded by the vicissitudes of life—the roller coaster ride of pleasure and pain, gain and loss, praise and blame, fame and obscurity—often requires a substantial depth of patience if one is to experience a sense of balance and joy in this precious life.

The development of patience requires an understanding of the root causes of our stress, anxiety, and frustration. Then we must be willing to relinquish the type of thinking that leads to the loss of patience. Although anger and patience are not opposites, they can be thought of as two sides of the same coin. When one side is visible the other is hard to see. When one side is active the other is unlikely to emerge. That does not mean that the patient person does not experience anger, or that the person easily disposed toward anger never displays great patience. Indeed, the most advanced spiritual practitioner remains human and continues to experience human thoughts, feelings, and sensations. However, the development and continuing practice of patience can prevail so that one does not respond in conditioned ways or with emotional reactions that can cause suffering to oneself and others. In the Buddhist tradition the vehicle for this kind of spiritual growth is called *mindfulness*. We will look in depth at the quality of mindfulness, but for now we can think of it as a moment-to-moment, nonjudgmental, nonclinging, engaged level of awareness. It is mindfulness that enables us to sense the arising of feelings and emotions such as impatience and anger at their initial stirring and to calmly invite patience to come to the fore. Because of anger's enormous potential for danger, it would not be an exaggeration to say we call on patience to come to the rescue, to save the day, perhaps even to save a life.

As we journey through these pages we will explore various aspects of everyday living that can challenge the patience of the most well-intentioned among us. Don't worry about finding opportunities to practice. Rest assured that someone or something will show up to test how well your patience is developing. There is a small plaque in the guest bathroom of a friend's house that reads, "God give me patience, and I mean right now!" Unfortunately, it doesn't happen that way. One thing we will surely see is that it takes patience to develop patience.

To get a broader view of people's everyday experiences related to patience I asked hundreds of people of varying ages, locales, occupations, ethnicities, and interests two questions: (1) Under what condition(s) are you most likely to lose your patience? and (2) When that happens, what do you do? While this was not intended to be an in-depth, scientific research project, certain tendencies emerged quite clearly: a major cause of impatience seems to be people feeling they are not being heard (sometimes stated as feeling ignored). Another is people feeling their space is being invaded or not being respected. Other frequently mentioned causes of impatience were fatigue, hunger, technology failures, rude behavior, and feeling rushed. As to what people do to regain their patience, mentioned most frequently were various practices of conscious breathing and, when possible, distancing oneself from the source of annoyance. Some people's specific responses appear herein at the end of various chapters.

The first and last chapters focus on two concepts I have found to be essential if we are to experience any sort of spiritual and/or emotional growth. They are so powerful and limitless in their potential that I think of them as sacred. The first chapter, *Start-*

ing Patiently, addresses the first of these two concepts: an aspect of the law of inertia; things that are stationary tend to remain so. That which is weighed down, including our thought processes, can be stubbornly, fearfully resistant to initiating the effort that leads to growth and development. So we will look at our innate resistance to change, and explore ways to move gently through the obstacles to opening up and gaining greater insight into truth and reality. The courageous act of starting to address one's anger and develop greater patience is, to me, a sacred act. In the last chapter, *The Art of Peaceful Living*, we will learn how the second concept, a pause, invites the mind and body to stop, to allow fiery thoughts to cool and subside before giving them expression. It allows the time and spaciousness needed for compassionate and wise thought. Therefore, we will see how the practice of pausing opens the door to new beginnings. We will examine a multifaceted practice for developing a depth of patience so that it becomes part of who we are.

For many, the most difficult person with whom to be patient is oneself. We often graciously forgive others and praise their good intentions even if the results of their efforts prove less than satisfying. Yet when we ourselves slip up and speak or act poorly we can routinely find our actions deplorable and oftentimes unforgivable. Patience with oneself is essential if we are to enjoy happiness and equanimity through life's constantly changing nature with its unfair and disruptive conditions. If we are not patient with ourselves it is unlikely that we can be patient with anyone else. Conversely, it is not surprising that as we develop patience with ourselves we will find it easier to be patient with others.

In the Buddhist tradition wisdom is said to arise when we

see things as they really are, not as they appear to be. Yet to transform our usual views, opinions, and perceptions so that we can see the true nature of things can be a challenging process. It is a part of our journey that can require great patience both with ourselves and with others. Wisdom is all too often painfully earned. As Confucius said, "By three ways do we attain wisdom. The first is by contemplation, which is the noblest; the second is by imitation, which is the easiest; the third is by experience, which is the bitterest." Seeing things as they really are, rather than through the distorted lens of conditioned perception, can be challenging to the intellect as well as to our patience.

We have much less control than we might think over the causes and conditions that converge to bring about the ever-changing circumstances of our lives. The events of every moment come about from the contingent factors that precede them. Nothing exists by itself; everything is interconnected. We can often see the short-term connections, but the bigger picture, the universal law of cause and effect known as *karma*, is often obscured to the untrained, unfocused mind. With practice we can learn to put full effort into our actions without our happiness being dependent upon the ensuing results. To do this requires a clear understanding of our intention as well as insight into the connected nature of all phenomena.

Over time most of us learn that fame, power, and a bulging purse may bring with them a certain pleasurable boost as well as freedom from financial stress (not insignificant), but since all things change there is no lasting delight in external possessions. Joy must be developed from the inside. If we cannot find happiness within ourselves we will not be able to find happiness anywhere.

Our lives are lived in relationship with others. That is why Buddhist teachings place such emphasis on the way we speak with one another. Probably nothing could improve the quality of our relationships as quickly as even one moment a day spent in greater awareness of the words we speak. This is how we develop *skillful speech*, a revered quality among wise beings. Yet to stop and pay attention to our own words when those of another appear rude, abusive, or hurtful can require the patience of a saint, or at least that of an astute, compassionate being. When the views of another are different from our own we can feel impatient or threatened. To listen with an open mind and heart is an invaluable skill that takes time and effort to develop.

Our most intimate and loving relationships are the very ones that can frequently try our patience. We share our most treasured time with our loved ones. We make our biggest decisions together. We face life's challenges as partners. We're not always going to see things the same way. Our children will certainly not see the world as we do. From infancy to the difficult teen years and indeed throughout life, our relationships with our children will require patience. It can be of some solace to realize that they must be patient with us as well. For our home to be a refuge it needs to be a place where love, compassion, and patience prevail.

The workplace is one area where a person trying to diminish the harmful effects of anger and backbiting chatter can find things tough and chewy, meaning too many mouths may be spewing too much malice. The workplace is, for many, where we spend most of our day, both physically and mentally. It occupies our mind from the time we wake up in the morning and choose our outfit for the day to the persistent, lingering thoughts that remain even as we rest our head on the pillow for our nightly slumber. We may need to accommodate an irritable boss or coworker while feeling overworked and underappreciated. Gentle but firm patience needs to be employed so that we can coexist with those who often bring to the workplace a bleak view of the world.

We have become more and more reliant on the technological marvels that connect our thoughts and words with all humanity. PCs and laptops, cell phones, printers, copiers, and tablets function flawlessly most of the time and we pretty much take them for granted. However, when they falter, which always seems to happen when we are in the middle of a project that "can't wait," we are introduced to an opportunity to find out how our practice of patience is coming along. Little will be accomplished without a balance between patience and perseverance: a healthy mixture of "All good things come to he who waits" and "He who hesitates is lost" seasoned with a dash of "This too shall pass" and a soupçon of "A rolling stone gathers no moss."

Imagine, if you will, a gigantic mountain several miles high, say about three times the height of Mount Everest. Now imagine a bird gently gliding by with a flowing silk scarf dangling from its beak. Once every hundred years the bird flies over the mountain and the silk scarf brushes across the mountaintop. According to Buddhist lore, the mountain will be completely worn away by the scarf in less time than the completion of one *kalpa*. The Sanskrit word kalpa means an "eon," or an extremely long period of time.

The word appears in ancient Hindu and Buddhist teachings and, in more contemporary times, in *Guinness World Records*, where the 4.32 billion year kalpa is listed as the longest measurement of time. The exact accuracy of these figures notwithstanding, you get the idea that a kalpa, or eon, is a heck of a long time.

The eighth-century Indian scholar and philosopher Acharya (teacher) Shantideva cautioned that one moment of anger, a moment when we lose our patience, can destroy the good that we have accumulated over many kalpas. This view, extending as it does for an essentially incalculable time frame, assumes that we are reborn many times, but whether or not we believe in rebirth is not significant. Be it in one lifetime or many, we are all familiar with the enormity of the destructive power Shantideva ascribes to words and deeds born of impatience. He says, further, that anger, like no other force, leads to grief, sadness, despair, and suffering. Who among us would disagree? Have we not been in relationships that we cherished only to see them severely damaged, perhaps irreparably, by a single outburst of anger? Healing the damage caused by just one such eruption can take months or even years. We can adamantly cling to our anger for decades with no sense of the hurt we are inflicting upon ourselves and others. Shantideva offers the view that once we see the uselessness of holding on to our anger we are well on our way to overcoming it. In a sense, patience is both the tool for, and the result of, our efforts. We will need patience to overcome the powerful habit energy of anger and irritability. Patience is our ally as we endeavor to undermine the energy of anger. The emergence of greater patience is the gift we receive each time we're victorious in even the smallest bout with ill will, annoyance, and irritation. In the chapter *What Would a Sage Do?* we learn what Shantideva taught himself about overcoming anger and impatience.

While preparing this project I met with several people whose life circumstances have required them to develop an extraordinary depth of patience: Michael Naranjo, a renowned Native American sculptor who was blinded and maimed in the Vietnam War; Lisa, who faced a heart-wrenching challenge she could never have anticipated; Venerable Metteyya, a Nepalese monk who deals with painstakingly slow circumstances while trying to change untenable conditions; and Noël Carmichael, a young woman who uprooted her life and went to Tanzania in an attempt to save the lives of thousands of children. Their stories appear as *Profiles in Patience*.

To be present to what is happening within and around us moment to moment is to be fully engaged in life. Without the ability to be present we are missing much of what the adventure has to offer. The mind moves so quickly from an actual event as it is happening, to our construct of the event that we rarely take in the authentic, bare experience. We know only our perceptions, which we accept as reality. Training the mind to be mindful is for most of us an ongoing and deeply rewarding process. In the various Buddhist tracts there is considerable emphasis on the development of concentration, not to empower one to be able to bend a spoon with our minds, or to walk through walls, but rather that we might be able to develop and sustain a high level of precise focus. This type of concentration, called *single-pointed focus*, allows us to experience phenomena with greater clarity without the mind pulling us from thought to thought, feeling to feeling, sensation to sensation. It is not clouded by our likes and dislikes, which interfere with bare experience. Over time we become more present, moment to moment, in the actual events of our lives.

Inner peace can be seen as the ultimate benefit of practicing patience. It is that feeling of calm presence in the face of life's disruptions. The equanimous person is at the same time unattached yet deeply involved in life. She cares, she loves, she rejoices, she laughs, she cries, she feels deeply, and all the while she remains peaceful and calm.

At the end of each chapter there are contemplations for your consideration, and a practice to take into daily life. For the person interested in developing greater patience it is not enough to read about it. One must practice. Patience is a mental factor, so developing patience requires mental effort. Consider this book a guide, a companion as you do the work to develop greater patience. This work does not have to take a great deal of time each day, but it will require your intelligence, courage, and a sincere desire to become a more compassionate human being. You may also want to bring your sense of humor along on the journey. It often makes the best cushioning when a road gets bumpy.

At times our efforts may require gritty determination, for no spiritual journey is easy. Our dedication can be sustained by a deeper experience of the benefits of patience coupled with an ever-increasing insight into the destructive power of anger. It also helps to know that for many centuries countless beings have walked this path before us.

The engaged effort to overcome anger with patience reminds

me of a story from the Native American tradition. An elder Cherokee was teaching his grandchildren about life. He said to them, "A fight is going on inside me. It is a terrible fight between two wolves. One wolf represents anger, greed, hatred, envy, fear, arrogance, resentment, self-pity, guilt, lies, and ego. The other stands for peace, love, patience, joy, compassion, generosity, humility, kindness, friendship, truth, and faith. This same fight is going on inside you, and inside every other person, as well." The children thought about this for a while and then one child asked, "Which wolf will win?" The wise elder replied simply, "The one you feed."

A Few Words About a Word

The Pali[1] word *dukkha* is of utmost importance in Buddhist teachings. It is usually translated as "suffering," or, sometimes, "stress," or "dissatisfaction." In various contexts its many different translations are useful. The trouble is, the human experience has a seemingly limitless number of contexts and there is no single word in the English language that encompasses the vastness, profundity, and subtlety of this crucial term. In our culture we have a connotation of *suffering* that can be limiting. As an example, we tend to associate suffering with what Grandma went through in the last days of her life, or the feelings associated with the loss of a loved one, or the sensations of physical pain.

1. Pali: A Middle Indo-Aryan language of India; the language of many of the earliest extant Buddhist teachings, as in the Pali Canon.

These are forms of dukkha, but dukkha can also be very subtle, sometimes barely perceptible, yet present, manifesting as a mild uneasiness or slight discomfort. People in the midst of losing their patience are certainly experiencing an aspect of dukkha. Therefore, since no translation can ideally suit every situation, I have chosen often to simply use the word *dukkha*.

Starting Patiently

Patience: a virtuous quality characterized by calm endurance when dealing with difficult circumstances; perseverance when facing provocation or delay; not reacting negatively to annoyance or anger; forbearance when under stress, particularly that which is long-term; steadfastness when faced with difficulties; bearing misfortune or pain without loss of temper.

—Various sources

What is there about the quality of patience that causes so many of us to respond to the very word with a sense of deficiency? "I don't have enough, I need more," we say, putting it in the rarefied domain occupied by such phenomena as time and money. No matter how much money people have, they seem to feel they need more and, indeed, in difficult economic times, many truly do need more. As to time, in any given day we all get exactly the same amount. There's not much point in pleading for more because in each hour the clock offers only the allotted number of minutes and seconds agreed upon by our ancient ancestors. Grudgingly, it ticks with a relentless, unyielding persistence that alters not for even the most saintly or Buddha-like among us. The accepted measurement of time allocates twenty-four hours for each day, and for now and the foreseeable future, that is it. Unable to convince the clock of the joys of generosity that could be experienced by its offering just a bit more of its precious commodity, we alter our approach and try to squeeze just one more project into the day's already bloated schedule.

The wonderful thing about patience, unlike time, is the more we use it, the more we have. Also, by its nature, patience creates a spaciousness that lets us feel as if we have more time than we have ever had. Thus, patience can alter our everyday experience from one of anxiety and deficiency to one of peace and plentitude.

There are certain psychological advantages to residing within the same body for a lengthy period of time, say seventy years or so. For instance, when life's ever-changing nature presents itself in a particularly unpleasant form, it helps to know that we have been through it before, or something similar, and things have worked out. They may not have worked out exactly as we would have liked; nevertheless, they have worked out. We got drenched but the storm passed. There is something comforting about familiarity, even with that which is unpleasant. Familiarity can be a great ally in the development of patience.

By contrast, one doesn't tend to encounter many *physical* perks as the bodily structure ages. That is, unless you enjoy more frequent visits to doctors (who seem to be getting younger) as you experience various organs, muscles, neurons, and tendons beginning to show signs of extended use. Fortunately, most physicians are knowledgeable and caring, and by and large we get to live longer and healthier lives than our ancestors. The issue at hand is: Are we living happier lives and enjoying the calm serenity of inner peace? The Dalai Lama has expressed the view that we are here to be happy and, in my experience, most people seem to want to be happy. The obvious question then becomes: If we want to be happy, why do we so often act in ways that are in opposition to that end?

One of the major issues so many of us deal with is impatience—with ourselves, with others, and with an enormous range of situations. Anger and annoyance arise and we can lose our patience in an instant. Some of us have experienced so much impatience that we just assume we "do not have a lot of patience." (Why we refer to the virtuous quality of patience as if it were a commodity that can be measured quantitatively, I don't know. We'll address that as we go along.) We seem to believe that an emotional state is something that is embedded in us and that we can't free ourselves from it. The current vernacular suggests that we are "hardwired" a certain way and we cannot change. In truth, what happens is, we experience an emotion and then too often attach to it as if it were an innate aspect of our very being. Some of us label ourselves "an angry person," ignoring that the basic nature of sentient beings is more likely compassionate and kind, not angry and unpleasant. We allow ourselves to believe that anger and impatience are a part of who we are rather than understanding that they are simply feelings that arise. Like anything else that arises, feelings pass away. They do not define character. Repeated outbursts of anger and frequent loss of patience most likely indicate fear and unhappiness.

They are unpleasant to experience, but they are not fixed, permanent conditions. Again, it is important to remember that even if we frequently experience the arising of impatience or anger it does not define who we are.

I used to turn negative feelings into anger so that I wouldn't feel the pain of a hurtful situation. Of course I didn't know I was doing that, and the result was like fanning burning embers inside me. I would hold on to the anger, and consequently the suffering within me was never addressed. That is a potent recipe for anguish and despair, not to mention physical pain. For years I paid the price of loneliness even among loved ones and sadness in the midst of delight. It is through the development of mindfulness and patience that our more joyful nature has the opportunity to emerge. Over time we become sentient beings guided by well-honed wisdom and compassion. As we will see, even though we may need a little work, we are already whole and perfect. We may have lost touch with aspects of our perfection, but they are always there, just as the sun is always there, waiting for its chance to shine when the clouds have passed. As the sun waits patiently for a clear sky, we too can learn to be patient. This is the essence of spiritual practice; our work is not to become a better person, but to become present to the perfection we already are. That perfection may at times be a bit loony, shy, angry, righteous, or filled with self-doubt, but we still want to become friends with who we are. Just as the Buddha advised his followers to learn from their own experience, we too must pay attention to the messages from our own mind and body and learn what causes us dukkha and, alternatively, what brings peace and joy for ourselves and those around us. Then we make the wise decisions that determine our actions. We start with whatever patience we have; we can only start from where we are.

To begin an exploration of the practice of patience it is helpful to have a sense not only of what patience is, but also of what it is not. For example, when facing an intolerable situation such as two-year-old Jimmy's latest inexhaustible tantrum in a crowded supermarket, gritting your teeth and slowly counting to ten is not true patience. Likewise, while waiting on an interminable line, say at the airport security gate (which you suspect is not all that secure), consciously breathing deeply (and perhaps loudly so that the person you believe to be causing the line's comatose state can be made acutely aware of your annoyance) is also not true patience. These practices are more like techniques, skills used for getting through a challenging situation without completely "losing it." They employ qualities such as forbearance, tolerance, and endurance, and even if they feel forced or contrived they can put a bit of space between your feelings and your actions. They are a starting place and can be invaluable, although they are not yet the skills that will bring insight and advance us on the path to greater wisdom and inner peace. They do not emerge naturally from a well-practiced and skillfully developed quality of patience. That is because the development of genuine patience requires introspection over time so that we can come to know the root causes of our *im*patience.

Being mindful of the causes of our impatience we learn not to encourage them. We sense impatience, annoyance, and anger as they begin to arise within us and we then invite our calmer, wiser self to be present. Impatience and anger are natural feelings and we don't want to suppress feelings. However, we do want to be aware of our feelings as they arise so that we don't speak or act while fires are burning, a practice likely to cause misery for ourselves and others. We have to learn how to disagree without becoming annoyed and impatient. When we see the interconnected nature of all beings we realize that we are all in this together. There is nothing for us to defend. With practices like mindfulness, meditation, compassion, and lovingkindness we can transform our anger into more positive, productive energy. We learn how to create a pause, a sacred moment in time, between our feelings of frustration, of not being heard, seen, or understood, and our response to those feelings. As we want to be forgiven for our unskillfulness, we learn to graciously forgive others as well. The more patient we become, the more at peace we become. We see that patience is wise and compassionate. Without compassion and a willingness to forgive, the development of patience would be unlikely.

The destructive effects of anger are easily recognized. When even mild annoyance arises it can quickly grow and overwhelm us. Inner peace is lost. If we look at how anger arises we see that it usually happens when we feel unheard, unseen, or unfairly treated. If in that moment we look within, we may sense a feeling that anger can help us get even with the offending person or change the vexing situation. So the anger that arises can seem to have value, but in reality it cannot. There might be some logic to responding with anger if it could negate the offense that has taken place, but that cannot happen because the deed has already occurred. So anger cannot reduce or prevent the perceived wrong. In fact, if we react to a situation in an angry way instead of with patience, not only is there no benefit, but negative energy is created, which is likely to exacerbate a volatile situation. Further, when intense anger arises, it impedes our ability to use sound judgment and envision the consequences of our actions. Anger, annoyance, and impatience deplete energy. Patient effort strengthens our resources. We need to practice cooling emotional fires and alleviating fierce disruptions in our lives. The benefits of developing greater patience will be felt in all our relationships: intimate, casual, professional, as well as that all-important relationship, the one we have with ourselves.

The subtle process of mindfulness is a lifelong practice and most of us experience any number of slipups as we slowly progress. But with gentle, persistent effort, we stay the course. The serene and peaceful mind that is developed through mindfulness and reflection can find pleasure in its own patience. Those who think of patience as weakness and see anger as strength will be in for quite a revelation. In order for us to practice patience, we must have courage, wisdom, and a loving, compassionate heart. We must be wise enough to address disagreement with intelligence and thoughtfulness. We come to understand patience as noble and valiant. We discover that if we want to live in a more peaceful world we must develop a more peaceful world within. We must nurture love and compassion for ourselves as well as for other beings.

Khanti is the Pali word meaning "patience." Khanti refers to the practice of patience in the face of harsh, unkind, or abusive words or actions, or when dealing with delays or perceived incompetence. Khanti implies a genuine patience that arises with little or no effort and is offered graciously, rather than determined tolerance or fortitude while feelings of anger or resentment still simmer within us. At the same time, there may be instances where patience will have to remain a conscious choice, we hope made honorably, particularly in situations that "push our buttons" or in some way touch an easily offended part of us. However, over time even our most sensitive buttons can be disengaged.

In Buddhist teachings mindfulness is viewed as an essential aspect in the development of patience and, likewise, patience is invaluable for the development of mindfulness. Patience is characterized by an even-tempered perseverance and the capacity to move through challenging situations calmly and graciously. It is restraint when provoked and the capacity to experience difficulty, hardship, inconvenience, adversity, and stress while remaining calm and rational. This does not mean becoming a doormat for others to tread upon; quite the opposite. With patience we are more likely to see things as they really are and proceed with greater wisdom and compassion, making decisions that reflect the person we want to be. We gain the respect of others as they see us remaining poised and dignified in challenging situations. The person who has developed patience has a gracious, self-assured presence. In the modern vernacular, such an imperturbably serene person is *cool.* Patience in such a person is as natural as their height. They don't have to try to be their height, they simply are it. There may be times when we have to stand on our toes to reach a bit higher, but even that is done with ease. Just as it takes a number of years to grow to your full height, likewise the development of true patience, for most of us, will take time. Once developed, however, patience is a dependable, trustworthy ally.

When we cling to a desire for things to be different from the way they are, we are flirting with impatience because things *aren't* different than they are. They may not be fair, kind, or just, but they are as they are. In certain special circumstances if anger arises out of compassion related to an abusive or unjust situation it can become the motivation for wise action. If such action is intended to be beneficial, not vengeful, then anger with mindfulness can serve a positive purpose. But take note, anger arising from or fueled by hatred or a desire for revenge cannot be positive or beneficial. This is an important distinction.

If we are unhappy about a situation that can be changed, then we should do something to change it. However, if the situation cannot be changed, why waste time, effort, and energy being unhappy about it? Meditation teacher and author Sharon Salzberg puts it this way: "Impatience is feeling upset because things are not happening on our timetable, or wanting to be more in control of a process so that we can have something happen the way we'd like to see it happen. It's stepping out of a process in order to fret because something is not happening the way we would like to see it happen." Sometimes things just need to be accepted as they are, and accepted graciously if at all possible. If the situation is unacceptable, it is with compassion and wisdom that we look to make meaningful changes. If we cannot, there is no benefit to getting angry and letting our world become bleak. Despair and sadness can set in, the heart sinks, the body aches, and the mind closes off even from those we care about most.

Patience is supported and nurtured by a quality of forgiveness. Understanding that others, just like ourselves, are affected by stress, disappointment, and frustration is the first step toward being able to forgive, to let it go. Forgiveness of others becomes possible as we learn to forgive ourselves. When anger, resentment, bitterness, irritation, and other such feelings take hold of us, we can't enjoy peace or a feeling of ease. When others sense our anger, and they will, they can find it difficult to trust us. Thus, we create unrest not only for ourselves, but for those around us as well. On the other hand, when we begin to conscientiously overcome our anger, happiness and inner peace will be present more often.

Things usually become easier as we become more familiar with them. As we develop patience in dealing with life's inevitable little annoyances and disruptions, we discover that with our maturing skills we can also learn to handle life's greater challenges, such as serious illness, old age, and even death. That is not to say that we will enjoy pain and sorrow, but that we can learn to manage them with a calm and rational mind. While few among us like to be in unpleasant situations, they are part of life and they can provide some of our most valuable learning experiences.

The wise person is patient even in times of turmoil and disruption. We accept that there is nothing to gain by blaming others for our discomfort. Peace can be found within, no matter what the external circumstances. We can learn to be patient with others by developing compassion for ourselves. Our mind remains lucid, calm, and equanimous; thoughts, feelings, and sensations are seen for what they are—thoughts, feelings, and sensations—and are not mistaken for reality. It is even possible to see the benefits of discomfort. Without unpleasant and disruptive events we cannot learn patience. We might as well accept that view since it is the nature of life that we will experience dukkha. It is woven between the strands of joy and rapture. As we learn to practice compassion for ourselves we see that we are worthy of our love and kindness. Only by developing love and compassion for ourselves can we feel a true sense of love and compassion for others.

One thing I have learned over time is that if we cling to our feelings of anger, or worse, if we fan the flames of hatred, we are the ones who suffer. The person with whom we are angry may be affected for a moment or two, but no matter how much we rant and rave they go on with their lives. We are left with the fire burning inside. We lose sleep. We can't even enjoy a book, a movie, or a hot fudge sundae. As the Buddha said, "Holding on to anger is like grasping a hot coal with the intent of throwing it at someone else; you are the one who gets burned."

During these periods of anger, our ability to be productive, to do something beneficial for ourselves and others, is severely hampered. When we speak of fueling the fires of anger we are speaking of the "add-ons," the scenarios we create in our mind that flow so quickly and habitually from the initial feeling. We may experience anger because Janet has just spoken to us in an unskillful way. She appeared abrupt and dismissive. We feel hurt, but instead of being fully present to that hurt, aware that we feel sad, the mind makes a quick, almost imperceptible shift, and we feel angry. That anger then becomes justified as we create an image of Janet as a rude, arrogant person never caring one bit about what matters to others. It becomes impossible to imagine how we could ever have considered her a friend; she thinks only of herself. However, with mindfulness and a calmer presence we might remember that Janet said she was having a rough day and was late for an appointment. This is, after all, the same Janet who held your hand and provided solace and support during your divorce; who went an hour out of her way every day for two weeks to take you to and from work when your car was being repaired; and who watches little Cathy every week while you are in therapy. All that really happened was that Janet spoke abruptly. The serene mind sees that and understands. You let it go, or later, at an appropriate time and place, you speak with Janet. You explain that because you value your friendship and your honest relationship you want to address the hurt you felt when she said what she did. You do this with skillful speech and hope Janet understands, while also knowing that you cannot control her perceptions.

Years ago, when my previous marriage ended, I went through a period in which I felt as if I was always angry. The anger was so prevalent that, at times, I didn't even know where I was. I can remember one time crossing a busy street without looking or hearing the car horns blaring, and drivers yelling, "Are you crazy?" Actually, it was a legitimate question. In moments when we are totally consumed by anger it is as if we are experiencing a form of insanity. For a year I had trouble functioning. I didn't work much, I ate poorly, I was miserable to be around. As my teenage friends say, "Life sucked." I was nowhere near ready to examine the possibility that it might not have been life that was all screwed up, but that perhaps it was me. This was a time of feeling lost, unattractive, unloved, and totally unacceptable as a human being. Most of my friends were more comfortable with my ex, and I lost them as well. (I wonder why?) A weary yet persistent voice known as *mind* would speak to me about getting help. It reminded me that I didn't have to face this crisis alone. For many months the refrain kept trying to get my attention: "Get help." Another voice, known as *ego*, stoically countered, "You're a big guy—you'll be fine. Don't worry about the anger and the sadness." It took a long time for the truth to penetrate through my misery, but when it finally did, and I made the call to the person who would become my therapist for the next several years, I immediately felt as if the world had been lifted from my shoulders. The ensuing work was challenging, but it led to a significant turnaround in my career, a new and wonderful marriage, and my determined effort to become a more compassionate, joyful presence in the world. I can still clearly remember the moment in which I performed the sacred act of starting. Yes, starting is sacred because without it nothing great, nothing joyous, nothing meaningful happens. I also learned at that time that it helps to take your sense of humor along on the journey. Without it the road can be pretty rough. The great cellist Pablo Casals was asked why, at age ninety-two, he still practiced four hours a day. He replied, "Because I believe I'm making progress."

. . .

In practice we might find that our interest in developing greater patience is motivated by a longing for inner peace, a yearning for more meaningful relationships, or a sense of greater fulfillment in life. Buddhism views patience as having three aspects: forbearance or perseverance, endurance when stressed, and acceptance of truth. As mentioned earlier, perseverance is not true patience. It is more like the skills we develop that can get us through challenging moments—an interminable wait on the phone with the utility company, Uncle Fred's ubiquitous hurtful comments at Thanksgiving dinner, the insane driver who cuts you off and nearly causes your demise, and so forth. These are the "take a deep breath and count to ten" or "remember, this too shall pass" type practices that prevent us from causing (or perpetuating) suffering with a conditioned response or knee-jerk reaction. They keep us from making reactive comments or acting out while annoyed, actions that we would likely regret later on. While a gentle use of forbearance in a given moment may not feel authentic, it can be invaluable while we work to develop deeper levels of true patience.

With perseverance we learn to pause, and in that crucial moment a door to the heart can open and allow space for the arising of compassion. Understanding that others want to be happy, just as we do, and don't want to suffer, brings us in touch with our common humanity. We all slip and act poorly at times. Forgiveness of self and others arises more easily when we are in touch with our feelings and see clearly what triggered our anger. Otherwise, we can get caught up in justifying it, which does nothing to move us toward a sense of peace. The fire will continue to burn and we will be holding the hot coals.

Patience is born when we create a pause between our experience of a feeling and our response to that feeling. Without a pause we are likely to find ourselves reacting in our conditioned manner. After all, that is what conditioning is. With a pause there is at least the possibility of a more positive response, and certainly we are less likely to cause harm. Patience lives in the gap between our experience of an event and our response to that experience. If we spend time with our experience—the thoughts, feelings, and sensations that arise—we can gain insight. Wisdom arises as we see things with greater clarity. Forgiveness has space to develop; fires have a chance to cool.

When we see that the experience of sentient beings includes aging, illness, stress, and suffering, we can relax a bit and accept that it is the nature of things; it is the way things are. Perhaps if you or I had created the world things would be different, but for now this is it. This acceptance does not mean that we do nothing to alleviate dukkha. Quite the opposite. It means that we can be patient and then take action that is well considered, wise, and compassionate rather than reactive, unskillful, or vengeful. Patience, unlike popular misconception, is not characterized by passivity. It is alive, vital, and active. It is thoughtful and compassionate for one's self and others. We can look at things, including our own impatience, with a sense of curiosity and investigation, asking, "What is this?" rather than with a judgmental, dismissive view.

Both forbearance and endurance can help us avoid reacting with anger when we feel threatened or mistreated, or when the inefficiencies of others cause unnecessary delays. We can instead be mindful and take time to consider our response. Even a momentary pause can help us see more clearly, perhaps opening up a different perspective or an understanding of the other person's point of view. One of the tributaries of patience is compassion.

In Buddhist thought the beginning of wisdom is the ability to see things as they really are. Acceptance of truth relies on the development of wisdom because if we are to accept the truth, we must be able to recognize the truth. Discernment of truth, of course, is not always easy, which contributes to the challenge of developing true patience. It requires our taking the time to look beyond the surface to the deeper levels of our experience. We see that there is no self that has to be protected, inflated, or aggrandized. We do not have to defend some self-image that we have created. The ego may feel threatened, and *Mara*[1] (ego) can be a formidable opponent to spiritual growth. This is when patience is challenged at its deepest level. Here we must allow time to open a sense of spaciousness so that we ourselves become the fertile soil from which patience grows. Time is no longer an enemy; we do not feel rushed to react. Just as the Buddha looked right at Mara and calmly said, "I know you," and thus dissipated its power, we too can look directly at our fear and say, "I know

1. *Mara* is death in the form of the destroyer of spiritual practice. In Buddhist thought Mara is unskillfulness, temptation, and distraction from spiritual life. It makes the negative appealing and the positive not so. Mara embodies the desires that entrap and delude sentient beings. Mara is not so much evil as it is the power to seduce and negatively influence the unwary mind.

you. You are a feeling. You have no power unless I empower you and I choose not to do so."[2] As we see that defensiveness is unnecessary, we can then view a potentially confrontational situation with curiosity, interested in what is really going on with the other person. *Like me, he wants to be happy. Like me, she doesn't want to suffer. What can I do to ease this tension? Have I really heard his point?* With acceptance we have the time we need. We no longer have to rush in and change things. We can enjoy the opulent abundance of a patient mind.

Research is finding more and more evidence to suggest that we come into this life with varying degrees of virtuous character traits, such as patience, kindness, and compassion. One of the best-known studies involved young children—four-year-olds. It began in the late nineteen sixties with a professor of psychology in charge of the experiment. One at a time, the children were led into a room where they were shown a marshmallow on a desk. They were told they could either eat the marshmallow right away or, if they were patient and could wait a few minutes

2. Some 2,500 years ago, after trying many austere practices which did not bring him the enlightenment he sought, Siddhartha Gautama sat down beneath a fig tree, near the town of Gaya in northeastern India, and began to meditate. In his mind there arose a tremendous battle with Mara. Mara's power was great but Siddhartha's resolve was greater. Although Mara's forces were formidable and ferocious, Siddhartha remained calm and unshaken. Mara claimed that the seat of enlightenment should be his, not Siddhartha's. Mara's terrible forces supported him, exclaiming, "We are his witnesses." Mara demanded, "Who will speak for you, Gautama?" Whereupon Siddhartha reached down with his right hand and touched the earth and the earth roared its approval of Siddhartha. Mara was defeated. Siddhartha realized complete awakening and became a Buddha. He was not born an enlightened being but became one through his patient efforts and determination.

while the researcher was out of the room, they could have two marshmallows when he returned.

Films of these tests, which were conducted over several years, are moving, showing the children struggling, doing anything they could think of to be patient and resist gratification just a bit longer. Some covered their eyes or turned away so that they couldn't see the marshmallow. Others kicked the table or tugged at their hair or played with the marshmallow as if it were a toy.

The goal of the tests was to analyze the mental activity that enabled some people to be patient while others simply could not. Several papers were published but after a while interest in the experiment apparently faded. Then, years later the professor became aware of a relationship between the children's current development—they were now teenagers—and their patience as four-year-olds waiting to eat a marshmallow. He sent out a questionnaire to the parents, faculty, and counselors of the more than six hundred students who had participated in the experiment. He asked a wide variety of questions on topics ranging from the children's ability to plan ahead to their capacity to deal with challenging situations. He also examined their SAT scores.

The results showed that those who did not have the patience to delay gratification seemed more likely to have social issues and to struggle more in stressful situations. They also had trouble focusing on schoolwork. The children who had demonstrated greater patience with the marshmallow experiment had SAT scores considerably higher than the children who had shown less patience.

Previously, research had focused primarily on innate intelligence (IQ) as the most significant factor in predicting an individual's success. There is now evidence that raw intelligence alone is unreliable without testing the subject's ability to develop self-control. No matter how intelligent the child, she still must do what is required of her if she is to be successful at a particular endeavor. The marshmallow experiment put children in a situation where they had to figure out a way to make a specific circumstance work to their satisfaction. Even at this young age they were beginning to see that they had little control over the conditions in their lives, but they could control their perception of those conditions. With patience they could solve challenging issues. There also proved to be a significant number of children who didn't do well in the original marshmallow experiment, but had learned later on to develop patience and delay self-gratification.

More recent research was conducted with one thousand children, starting at their birth and continuing through their first thirty-two years. Results showed that the children who ranked lowest in patience and self-control, and who were easily frustrated, were approximately three times more likely to have multiple health issues, addictions, lower incomes, and commit crimes, than those with the most self-control. However, patience and self-control can be learned. The children in the study who worked on themselves showed marked improvement as they grew older. They reported a significant decrease in health and criminal problems compared with those who remained impatient and impulsive.

There is no question in my mind that the most impatient among us can, with calm effort and determination, overcome anger and impatience and lead happier, more satisfying lives.

CONTEMPLATIONS

It is worthwhile to train the mind,
which, because it is flighty resists control,
rushing about wherever it wishes.
A mind under control brings happiness.
Wise beings are mindful of their thoughts,
aware that they are delicate, tenuous,
and difficult to discern.
A mind well attended brings happiness.

—BUDDHA, THE DHAMMAPADA 35, 36

When angry we let others' mistakes punish us.
To forgive others is to be kind to yourself.

—MASTER CHENG YEN (TAIWANESE BUDDHIST NUN)

Practice

To become a truly patient person requires effort, and it will be difficult to sustain that effort unless you are genuinely motivated. Each day for one week, sit quietly for five minutes and consider your motivations for wanting to become more patient. Don't impose reasons on yourself because they seem "right" or because others think that way. Examine your personal experience. Look deeply at what matters to you. Reflect on your relationships, both personal and professional. How does your impatience or your anger affect your wife/husband/partner/children/friends? Be truthful with yourself: Would it be worth the effort to become more patient? At this point just ask the questions. Let the answers come when they are ready.

Patience with Self

Do not have doubts about the smallest good act, do not think, "Such an act will not bring happiness." Even as tiny drops fill the water jug, so the patient ones become filled with good, even though virtue may come slowly.

Buddha, The Dhammapada 122

For many of us the most difficult person with whom to be patient is ourself. Our pride, personas, and ego can feel disrupted and threatened every time we feel we have done less than our best. As mentioned earlier, Buddhists call this aspect of ego Mara, the enemy of spiritual growth. Mara exists within us all and seems to have a particular affinity for undermining patience. Mara opens the door and invites impatience to arise by diverting our eyes from truth and making it difficult to see things as they really are. When Mara gains a foothold in this way, patience can quickly be lost and irrational thoughts, words, and actions can emanate before we have a chance to think, or so it seems. When this happens we can so easily rationalize that we deserve our own annoyance. We speak to ourselves with a level of disrespect that we would rarely, if ever, inflict on another.

The reality is that there are times when we are unskillful. We simply don't perform up to our own expectations, the expectations of others, or our own self-image. Perhaps we didn't make the big sale the company was counting on, or we let the steaks burn to a crisp on the grill (again), or we had a bad day on the tennis court. We might have spoken to a loved one or a colleague in a manner we later realized was inappropriate or unkind. We would like to believe we are more skillful in our endeavors; we envision ourselves as more spiritually advanced, to the point where those slipups wouldn't happen. Yet they do, and we can feel deeply disappointed and annoyed with ourselves.

There are endless possibilities for becoming irritable and impatient with self, and in a given moment they can all seem absolutely justified. Thoughts arise: *I just did the same stupid thing again. How could I have said that? What a jerk. When am I going to learn?* Unfortunately, getting down on oneself rarely produces anything positive unless it happens to lead to determined resolve, which is difficult when the mind is bridled with self-criticism. Over time we see that just being impatient with ourselves rarely leads to anything beneficial and, in fact, the potential for harm, including devastating possibilities, can loom ominously close. Our emotional and mental states suffer. We may feel stressed and in despair which is often accompanied by a loss of self-esteem. In extreme circumstances serious depression may follow, requiring professional care.

When feelings such as anger and hatred arise they can be fueled by distortions and mental images that we create and accept as reality. The Buddha referred to this phenomenon as *delusion*. It can happen quickly and when it does objectivity is lost. We do not see things as they really are and thus wisdom cannot prevail. There is no quick fix for this unfortunate, but fairly common, pattern because rooting out an unskillful mental process requires time to objectively observe the mind's activity. Effort balanced with patience and a deep level of honesty with self are also necessary. For this, meditation is an ideal practice. In meditation we can bring to mind a situation that caused anger to arise. We then focus directly on the experience of that anger and its related thoughts, feelings, and physical sensations. There is no way to rush this process, we just stay with it. We keep returning to the thoughts, feelings, and sensations as they arise in the mind and body.

People sometimes say of themselves, "I'm not a good meditator." So what is a good meditator? A good meditator meditates. Beyond that, opinions among the world's masters vary enormously. I believe a teacher, a guide who has traveled the path longer than you have, can be helpful. Follow the teacher's advice regarding how often to sit and for how long. As progress is made the teacher will guide the subtleties of the practice. Don't be concerned about learning how to meditate. The practice is not something to learn. It is something to do. With the doing will come the learning.

We need to be patient regarding our progress. We cannot force the development of mindfulness. We must realize that growth is a process, and processes need their own time. We also don't want to compare ourselves with others. People progress at their own pace. We may not even know that we are making progress, but if we continue with gentle yet firm determination we will advance on our journey. Best-selling author Sharon Salzberg is one of the most renowned meditation teachers in the world, but her early experience learning meditation was not much different from that of the rest of us. She described it to me this way: "I experienced a lot of impatience. It was very difficult for me to concentrate my mind. I couldn't believe how challenging it was to do a seemingly simple thing like just keep my attention on the feeling of the breath. I thought, *How come everyone else can do this and I can't?* I just couldn't comprehend what was taking so long. I didn't understand that it was the actual unfolding of the path. I thought it was just me and that I had a problem, that I was aberrant. So I was very impatient."

We might think we will progress faster if we are ultra-self-critical, but be aware that impatience with self can easily become a form of self-hatred. People have said to me, "You don't understand, you're a Buddhist, you're don't lose your patience." If only that were true. By that logic a Christian would never get angry, nor would a Jew, a Muslim, or a Hindu. When we practice in a religious, spiritual, or philosophical tradition we're simply trying to live life a certain way. It does not mean we become Jesus, or the Buddha, or a saint, and we should not expect that of ourselves. The advanced practitioner is alive and experiencing thoughts, feelings, and sensations just like anyone else. The difference that comes with practice is how one responds to the challenges presented by life. Effective practice brings clarity and balance.

It is essential that we are patient with ourselves if we are to be happy, if we are to be trusted, if we are to be a welcome friend to others. It is deluding oneself to believe that we can be truly patient with others without first developing patience with ourselves. If we are to enjoy meaningful relationships, including the relationship with ourselves, patience must be developed to the extent that it is simply present and essentially unperturbed during trying situations. We are spiritual beings experiencing life in human form. As such, as one Zen master put it, we are perfect beings, *and* we need a little work. Among the qualities we can encourage within ourselves that will support that "little work" are acceptance, compassion, joyfulness, and generosity of spirit.

We must be willing to accept that we will make mistakes. A few years ago, a study of students in a university program looked to determine the qualities that separated those who did well in the program from those who did not. Two questions provided particularly valuable information: "Do you ever make mistakes?" "If so, what is the worst mistake you've ever made?" Those who did well admitted they made numerous mistakes and had already considered what they would do to not repeat those mistakes. More often than not those who did poorly answered that they rarely made mistakes and if they did, those mistakes were not their fault.

An easeful acceptance of our own slipups can begin by realizing that being human is not like being a machine that can be programmed to perfectly and repeatedly perform particular tasks. We are extremely complex beings and even those few among us who lead a relatively stress-free existence still are experiencing life within a body that is at the same time miraculous and vulnerable. That body is subject to illness, accident, decay, and death, each of which is a cause for dukkha. Finding the balance between gentle acceptance and the need for a skillful touch of increased effort is for many one of the ongoing challenges of daily life.

The complexity of human experience can truly be appreciated during the practice of meditation. It is then that one is alone with the mind, which can be a startling experience. If we ever questioned whether we have a relationship with ourselves, being left alone in silence with just the mind and body will end all doubt. It is here that we observe the way we speak to ourselves. Do we tend to be kind and compassionate or are we more often harsh and critical? Again from Sharon Salzberg: "If impatience is a strong habit in someone and they sit down to meditate, they will likely experience impatience, especially toward the practice itself."

Even the experienced meditator is often taken aback by how different the meditation experience can be from one moment to the next. Serenity can become turmoil which changes to bliss which gives way to fear, and on and on. We're tossed about as if we are but tissue paper in a breeze. In a recent three-month period a close friend of many years had a bicycle accident in which he broke his left clavicle and right wrist. Another friend had a skiing accident and broke her left leg. A neighbor was at dinner with her husband, when this athletic type in his mid-fifties had a heart attack and was pronounced dead moments later. Another neighbor discovered her teenage son, an excellent student, had a serious drug problem and had to be admitted to a rehabilitation program. During the same period, a friend finished a round of chemotherapy and was declared by her doctors to be cancer free. Another friend who had tried for years to get a novel published was offered a contract not only for that book but also for another yet to be written. A friend who had been out of work for a year was hired for a job he loves and is being paid more than he ever made before. I had a birthday and looked at the calendar with a sense of amazement. *Surely there's a misprint, where have all the years gone? Wasn't it just yesterday?* How can we not accept our little imperfections, even as we strive to improve? They are the beauty marks that enhance the splendid beings that we are. How can we not be patient with ourselves?

Meditation offers unique opportunities to learn about and practice patience with oneself. The first and possibly most important step in developing a meditation practice is to commit to sitting every day, or as close as you can to every day. Consistency is important. Here is your first opportunity to become impatient with yourself. See how you handle it. If you are new to meditation you may feel that on a given day you are too busy or too tired, or you might simply forget. None of these situations is ideal for building a meditation practice, so you might become annoyed or disappointed with yourself. The door is open for irritation, but this is also an opportunity to practice patience with yourself. At the same time you can calmly increase your determination. Perhaps you missed a session. It doesn't mean you're a slug or a slovenly, negligent, worthless dork. It means you missed a session. That evening or the next morning you simply do your next sitting. Decide on the time of day that you feel would be best to devote to meditation. You'll be less likely to miss a session as it becomes part of your daily life. Many meditators prefer the morning since it is often quieter and the day's activities have not yet begun to stir the mind. However, the time of day is not nearly as important as the commitment to practicing every day.

Some people begin their meditation sessions by setting an intention for the sitting. It may be something like, *May I become more mindful that I may be of benefit to myself and others*, or simply, *May I be patient in this sitting and throughout the day*. If you do begin with a stated intention, do so by being fully focused on it so that you develop a sense of commitment to your intention. Many Buddhists begin by taking refuge: *I take refuge in the Buddha, I take refuge in the Dharma, I take refuge in the Sangha.* This refers to the Three Jewels of Buddhism. Buddha, the teacher, in this context can be a symbolic reminder that he was a human being just as we are and he was able to become an awakened being and live without creating dukkha. (The fully awakened Buddha was still a human being and, as such, experienced illness, injury, and old age but he experienced these conditions from a perspective that did not create suffering.) The *dharma* refers here to the teachings of the Buddha, and the *sangha* is the community of noble beings who have traveled this path before us. The sangha can also refer to any group of people who study the dharma and practice meditation together.

If you are new to meditation you might want to start with sittings of a modest length, even five minutes is fine; you have nothing to prove. In the beginning five minutes can seem like an eternity. Facing an hour of an activity that may present physical, mental, and emotional challenges is not inviting and certainly not likely to elicit an enthusiastic return to your next sitting. Again, the important thing is consistency. With time, your concentration will become more focused and your body will adjust. There is no ideal length of time for sitting although many teachers suggest working your way up to thirty or more minutes. This might seem like a major commitment, and it is, but you are always free to choose your priorities. Remind yourself at the start of each session that your purpose is to alleviate suffering, for yourself and those around you.

Select a specific place for your daily practice. Turn off the phones, radio, television, and any other electronics that could interrupt your concentration. If there are others at home let them know that you would like not to be disturbed during your meditation time. You don't need an entire room for your practice. A corner with a table or bureau on which you can place a fresh flower, candle, book, photo, or anything that you find inspiring will do, although none of these are necessary. Your chair or *zafu* (meditation cushion) should be nearby as well.

The traditional lotus sitting position (one foot resting on the opposite thigh and the other foot on the other thigh) is usually not comfortable for most Westerners to maintain, especially those over five years of age. A particular position does not by itself make one a better meditator. The Buddha taught that the proper positions for meditation are sitting, standing, lying down, and walking. You want to find a comfortable position in which you can be both relaxed and alert, a position you can maintain without moving for the duration of the sitting. If sitting on a meditation cushion is not comfortable, a chair is fine. There are also meditation benches on which one sits/kneels during the session. Whatever posture you choose, have your back straight. Sit in a dignified manner. If sitting on a chair, be slightly forward so that you are not leaning back against the chair. Let your hands find a comfortable position where they can remain without moving throughout the sitting. Some traditions emphasize specific hand positions, but if you are not practicing in one of those traditions I think it is fine to allow the hands to be where they would like to be. Eyes can be closed or open. If open, take a soft focus toward the floor about six feet in front of you. An advantage to the eyes being closed is that there is one less sense door, sight, for distractions to enter. Some traditions teach that the eyes should be open, so you begin to get the idea that in many aspects of meditation you have choices. Feel free to experiment, but give each of your choices enough time so that you can learn about them. Again, the one point that is emphasized in most systems is the need for consistency. Practice each day if at all possible.

You can start your sitting with a body scan beginning at the top of the head, quietly noticing any stress or tension as you move your awareness slowly down through the body. Do this without judgment or self-criticism. You deserve to be happy; you didn't purposefully create stress or tension. Get a sense of what it is like to experience the sensations of being within a body. You could also start by bringing your awareness to sound. There are very few places on earth where there is no sound whatsoever. Just hear sound. There is no need to identify the sound. Notice, if you have preferences, sounds you like and those you dislike, and see if you can let those preferences go, and just hear sound. Sound is simply vibration. Attractions (likes) and aversions (dislikes) are created by you. They are not inherent in the sound.

Now bring your awareness to what is traditionally called an *object of concentration*, such as the sensations of the breath. You can note these sensations at the nostrils, abdomen, chest, or wherever works best for you. The object of concentration will be your anchor during the sitting, that to which you return when you become aware that your concentration has wandered. When concentration does wander, simply return to the sensations of the breath without criticism or judgment. Drifting of the mind from thought to thought is to be expected. You are experiencing the nature of the untamed mind. Direct your awareness back to the sensations of the breath. Each time you notice that the mind has wandered is a moment of mindfulness and is viewed as a most important moment in meditation practice. If you have to come back a thousand times in one sitting, that's fine. Your gentle yet firm determination is what matters, not how often the mind wanders. Over time your concentration will strengthen, but it does take time. This is when your patience and practice of meditation can support and complement each other.

The body knows how to breathe; from your first day it has been doing so and, except for an occasional illness, it has done so effortlessly. Then when we begin to practice awareness of the breath something happens. We seem to want to help, to make shallow breaths deeper, shorter breaths longer, and so forth. This may be because we become conscious of the self as the breather, a type of self-consciousness that turns a perfectly functioning body into a container filled with stress, concern, and doubt. What was intended to be simple awareness can become a self-conscious tangle. Remind yourself that there is nothing to fix. In fact, there is nothing to do at this point but observe what is going on. Allow yourself to just *be*. You may be so psyched to always be doing something that you have become a human *doing*. Now you will take the time to be a human *being*.

Nothing can come up in meditation that is not already inside you. No thoughts or feelings penetrate from outside ourselves. Our anxieties, heavy and light, related to daily functioning are likely to appear at some point as we practice. As an example, if we are trying, subtly or otherwise, to control the breath, we may be able to learn something about how we handle control issues in our everyday activities. Meditation is then a perfect opportunity to practice relinquishing control and letting the body do what it has done beautifully for years.

There are very few activities in life about which it can be said that there is no "right" way to do them. Breathing is one of those activities. (This is assuming that the breathing process is not being interfered with by an illness.) What a joy it is, not having to fix something, to make it better, to improve it. If you have certain beliefs that your breathing should be done this way or that, you can let all of that go. Again, the body knows how to breathe. Our practice is about mindfulness of breathing, which means just observing and noticing with interest and curiosity.

What we will observe is that the breath may be long, deep, short, or shallow. It may feel free and easy or it may feel rough and constricted. There is no need for concern and no reason to change anything. Just be mindful of what is happening as it is happening. With careful observation we begin to notice the subtle differences in the sensations of each breath. Therefore, what we observe in this session may seem quite different from what we noted in the last and what may well be in the next.

Sometimes we become more aware of our self than we are of the breath. It is difficult to imagine that the process happens without a "breather" steering the ship. Yet, over time, as we become more at peace, calmer, more focused, we learn to simply let the breath breathe. This deeply personal experience, this absorbed concentration, will likely require patience to develop.

What is most important is your intention to be present, free of expectations and concerns. Observe and accept whatever arises and know that everything is as it needs to be. Direct your gentle effort toward being present and noticing whatever is. If you have heard others speak about the potential benefits of meditation it can be easy to find yourself looking for blissful experiences. It rarely happens that way. There can be peacefulness and joy in a particular sitting, but the deeper benefits are more likely to unfold over time.

In the early stages it can be astonishing to observe how the mind wanders from thought to thought. Memories from long ago meld into visions that reach far into the future as the mind recalls what was and fantasizes about what is yet to be. Directing the mind to stay in the present can be a formidable task. People often think that the mind suddenly becomes hyperactive when they sit down to meditate. The term *monkey mind* aptly describes the phenomenon. In truth, while meditating we are simply seeing what the mind has been doing all along, only now we are taking time to observe, to be mindful. Remember, no thoughts or feelings will come up in meditation that are not already within you.

Doubt can be a powerful hindrance to meditation practice, raising anxiety and causing impatience. *I can't do this. This is not for me. I have more important things to do,* are thoughts familiar to many meditators. Try to remember that they are just thoughts, not reality. As such, they have no power other than the energy you give them. Observing your thoughts, feelings, and sensations is the grist of the practice. They are what is happening in the moment. It can help to remember that you do not have to believe everything you think. In meditation our practice is to watch our thoughts with a light heart and keen interest. As we learn to do that, we actually are able to see thoughts and feelings as they arise and then fade away. That is what all phenomena do, they arise and they fade away. Thoughts, feelings, and sensations arise constantly; it is the nature of the mind/body experience. When we learn to see them simply as thoughts, feelings, and sensations, they lose their power to pull us into negative emotional states or to react with knee-jerk, potentially harmful, conditioned responses.

Research has shown that a thought, if we only observe it, has a very short life span, barely more than a few seconds. Thoughts and feelings appear to have lasting power because we attach onto them and create scenarios based on our emotional responses to them. Let's say we look outside our office window and see that it is a bright sunny day. We smile and think, *What a beautiful day. Look at the kids running around and having a great time. I wish I could be out there with them instead of in here with Excel spreadsheets, stupid lists, clients' orders, and all this other crap. Where's the sunshine in my life? I never even get one minute of fun. My life sucks!* Versions of that short scenario are familiar to many of us. However, the only reality in that story is that the sun is shining and children are playing. The rest is the way that we choose to experience the sunshine. Of course the story could be written an infinite number of ways, but each version is only an "add-on" to the sunny day. In other words, the sunshine itself has no meaning except for that which each of us gives it. So it is with all things. We create our experience of life with our thoughts. Doesn't it then make sense to become intimately familiar with our thought process, and doesn't it also make sense to encourage thoughts that bring happiness and discourage those that bring unhappiness?

Aside from the many physical, mental, and emotional benefits of meditation, I can't think of a more effective practice for developing patience with oneself. Sometimes we experience sleepiness or restlessness during our sitting. When that happens we can become self-critical. A more beneficial choice might be to try an alternative: walking meditation. It can be joyful and beneficial to take a leisurely stroll in the park or on the beach, experiencing the natural sights, smells, and sounds. Certainly do that as often as possible. However, that delightfully refreshing walk is not the same as walking meditation, which too can be joyful and rejuvenating. Walking meditation is a specific practice that brings mindfulness to the physical movements of the body. You will need a space long enough to take at least ten full strides in a straight line. Since your steps will become very slow as you move through the practice, it might be wise to walk where you can have some privacy. The very slow walk can look somewhat strange to those who are not familiar with the practice.

When the weather is mild I practice walking meditation in a fairly private area outside of my New York City apartment. I'm sure the neighbors who can see me must think I'm rather strange or recovering from surgery, if not both. Years ago, when I first learned walking meditation I was practicing with the Vietnamese Zen monk Thich Nhat Hanh on a college campus in Vermont. There were some six hundred of us there on retreat and we would start early in the morning, leaving the dorm area and walking very slowly up a hill to the meditation hall. The morning air was cool and foggy, and it was an extraordinary vision in the first light of day to see all those bodies barely moving ever so slowly up the hill. It looked as if the ground itself was undulating As cars drove by I'm sure the drivers must have thought they were witnessing the weirdest cult gathering ever assembled. For me it was the beginning of my love and appreciation of walking meditation.

Begin your session by walking at a fairly brisk pace, first in one direction and then back the other way. Hands can be at your sides, clasped behind your back, or folded in front of you at the waist. Once you begin walking leave the hands where they are, no scratching or nose-wiping (which can become quite interesting on a day when you have a runny nose). Continue in this way for a few minutes, bringing a gentle awareness to the body and in particular to the movement of the legs and feet. Now slow down to a normal pace and increase your awareness of the specific movements of the feet. After several minutes slow down to a pace where you can become quite mindful of the steps you are taking. With each step add a quiet mental note, *Step, step, step.* Be particularly mindful of the movements of the feet as you stop, turn, and change direction. Continue this way for a few minutes, reminding yourself to be mindful of the movements of each step. Then slow way down, to a pace that is so slow that you can mentally divide the movements of each step into three parts. As you slowly move each foot, let this thought be in the back of your mind: *Lift, forward, down. Lift, forward, down.* Each time the foot touches down, let that foot be the primary support for your weight and when you feel steady, slowly move into the next step: *Lift, forward, down.* Even though the pace is slow, the actual movement of the feet should be the same as your normal step—no exaggerated movements. This slow movement is the main part of your walking meditation and can be continued for as long as you like, but for at least five minutes. As in sitting meditation, when the mind wanders come back to the object of concentration, which in this case is the movement of the legs and feet. Unlike sitting meditation, walking meditation is obviously done with the eyes open, looking a few feet in front of you.

An alternative form of walking meditation is to coordinate the breath with the steps. You again start with a fairly brisk pace, counting four steps per in-breath and four per out-breath. To slow down, you count three steps per in-breath and three per out-breath. Then two, and eventually one breath per step, which creates a very slow pace. Again, the focus is on the physical movements, with the counting of the steps done lightly in the background of the mind.

I can remember that as a child I would sometimes count my steps in an unconscious manner as I was walking. That habit stayed with me so that when I was learning walking meditation I would notice the mind counting. This unconscious counting is not a form of meditation, and I had to use mindfulness and determination to overcome that stubborn old habit. There is, however, a form of counting that can be used effectively as a meditative practice. You count your first five steps, then count backward to one. Then count again, up to six, then count back again to one. Then count to seven and back again to one, and then up to eight and back to one, then to nine and back to one, and then to ten and back to one. At that point go back to five and start the process again. The mind is focused since it requires concentration to keep track of where you are in the counting.

I don't recommend this as a main walking practice, but it is good to have alternatives if practice feels stale.

When I first started practicing walking meditation I had trouble with balance. I would often stumble to one side or the other. After a while I began to sense that my lack of balance was coming from some subtle resistance to moving slowly. Perhaps my big-city, fast-paced mentality plus years of conditioning were not comfortable with the slow, fully present nature of the meditation. My body seemed to have some impatient desire to "get there." However, in walking meditation there is no "getting there." You are already there; you are where you are. There is only "here," where you are right now. The body learns to be patient; the mind learns to be present. You are exactly where you need to be.

In *vipassana* (insight) meditation we come to see that every thought, feeling, and sensation that arises then passes away. All phenomena are impermanent. When practicing meditation we can see this more clearly because we lay aside all other activities and focus our attention on the activity of the mind. No matter how pleasant or unpleasant a thought or sensation may be, it will pass away and we can observe that passing as it happens. We can, with patience and practice, learn to observe the entire cycle of arising and passing away.

A physical sensation, no matter how pleasant or unpleasant we may perceive it to be, is simply a series of vibrations. They arise and they pass away. In Pali, the impermanent, ever-changing nature of things is called *anicca*. When we see for ourselves the reality of anicca, we are gaining insight into the way things really are. This experience can help change our conditioned way of thinking.

Understanding that everything is impermanent, we don't need to react with our usual craving for more of what we find pleasant, or with desire to push away or escape from that which we find unpleasant. This is the ground of equanimity and inner peace.

> I have observed over the past few years that as I have become less arrogant, I have become more patient. I am beginning to understand how the fear I have lived with all my life has generated all the stuff that has in turn given rise to impatience. So I now believe that what makes me lose my patience is my own fear.
>
> —AN AUTHOR FROM SOUTH DAKOTA

The Body

On the morning of my last birthday I jotted down these words:

> Who is the demon that keeps turning the pages of my calendar?
> Sometimes I catch a glimpse of him in his long black shroud,
> straggly white beard to his waist, curved sickle in hand,
> always checking the time
> on some complex clock strapped to his bony wrist.
> I'm just a kid.
> How can I be approaching an age that no one
> in my family has ever reached?

There are phenomena on this planet, such as the mountains and the oceans, that are so immense and change so gradually that it can be difficult to believe they are changing at all. On the other hand, one of the most obviously changing marvels available for our observation is the very body inside of which we are experiencing life at this precise moment. The only trouble with that is, who among us is truly enthralled with the changes we see happening to our bodies? Any delight we might have taken in the evolving of our bodily parts probably ended by the time we were twenty or after our first six months at the gym. For many, the physical body is a source of distress no matter how perfectly acceptable the rest of the world deems it to be.

I recently asked a roomful of meditators how many were happy with their body exactly as is and wouldn't change one thing about it. There was then a roomful of smiling meditators and considerable laughter, but no one raised a hand. Diets to gain or lose weight are part of the American way of life. If diets don't work fast enough there are drugs to stimulate or depress various glands and organs, supposedly leading to weight gain or loss at a more rapid pace. Skilled surgeons have busy schedules making body parts larger, smaller, firmer, or rounder. Yet the body continues to age and will eventually die. No scalpel can cut through reality.

Our relationship with the body we inhabit will last the entire length of our life. Wouldn't it make sense to become friendly with, and well-disposed toward, that which is always, literally, around us? Without an attitude of graciousness, or at least acceptance, we may find ourselves living in a state of low-level dissatisfaction and impatience. Sometimes we may be too busy to notice, but other times we may feel downright disgusted with our appearance. With the commercial world bombarding us with reasons to be dissatisfied with our face and form, it can be difficult to appreciate the beauty of our being as is.

Comparing yourself to others is meaningless. Focus on the beauty of you. Let there be a lightness about your being. See the bizarre nature of the things we do in our pursuit of happiness. Lightness encourages patience. As e. e. cummings said, "The most wasted of all days is one without laughter."

Having now spent a significant number of years in one body I can speak from experience of the joys and challenges of aging. Graying hair never bothered me; I think it looks rather sophisticated—in fact on some I find it absolutely stunning. On the other hand, I remember the first time I noticed that the skin on my arms was not as tight as it used to be. My first thought was that I would immediately have to increase my workout time. I soon learned that was not going to work, nor could I do much to tighten the skin that was loosening around my neck. This is the natural aging of the body. I've actually come to find some joy in the process. After all, I've spent quite a few years earning my wrinkles. The end of the aging process will come soon enough so I choose to enjoy it while I can.

Wisdom evolves from seeing things as they are and patience comes from accepting things as they are. If a situation is unacceptable and we can do something to change it, we should do so. If not, it is wise to accept life's conditions. In the Upajjhatthana Sutra,[1] the Buddha teaches: "This body is of the nature to grow old; I cannot avoid aging." No matter what creams, drugs, or surgeries we may bring upon ourselves, the body is aging. We have

1. "Subjects for Contemplation."

the opportunity to grow in wisdom as we age, or we can resist what is natural and struggle to the finish line. It has been shown to be beneficial to eat well, exercise regularly, and practice good health, physically, mentally, and emotionally. Then be patient with what is. Your unhappiness will not slow the aging process. In fact, there is evidence that suggests the opposite.

Life within a body involves sickness, old age, and death. That is natural order: what is subject to birth is subject to decay and death. We need to be patient with the body and with the reality of aging. Peace arises as we accept that which is. Aging and death are not punishments, nor are they phenomena we do or do not deserve. They occur because they are conditions of life.

> If I am overwhelmed, then even the tiniest disruption can trigger a disproportionate and utterly irrational meltdown.
>
> —A NEW YORK ACTOR

Impermanence

The Buddha taught that there are three universal characteristics of existence. These three characteristics are at the core of all phenomena[2]: *anicca,* the characteristic of impermanence; *dukkha,* the characteristic of unsatisfactoriness; and *anatta,* the characteristic of not-self. We use the term *characteristic* to describe something

2. Technically, all *conditioned* phenomena. According to the Buddha all phenomena arise due to causes and conditions (the doctrine of *paticcasamuppada*). This is called the *law of conditionality* or *dependent co-arising.*

that is always part of something else—let's say, as heat is a characteristic of fire. When there is fire there is heat. A characteristic helps us know something about the phenomenon of which it is a part. To understand the characteristic of impermanence is to understand something profound about the reality of our existence. Specifically, everything changes; everything *is* changing. All things that arise will fade away; all things have a limited existence. (It is part of human perception that things we find pleasant seem have to a shorter existence while things we find unpleasant seem to have a longer existence.)

At almost the same time as the Buddha, the Greek philosopher Heracleitus (ca 535 BCE–475 BCE) was offering his doctrine of change, which he saw as being central to the universe: "You cannot step twice into the same river." (Or: "No man ever steps in the same river twice, for it's not the same river and he's not the same man.") "Everything flows, nothing stands still." "Nothing endures but change." (Or: "The only constant is change.") Without a realization of the impermanent nature of all things, we cannot experience wisdom because we cannot see things as they really are. Heracleitus also said, "Abundance of knowledge does not teach men to be wise."

Unnecessary disappointment, despair, and frustration, which can give rise to impatience, often originate from not accepting the laws of nature. It is therefore important for us to understand the nature of impermanence. Understanding helps us accept the look and feel of our aging body. It helps us reduce tensions in our relationships and live happier lives in harmony with nature. That includes the nature of things that are not always the way we would like them to be. But let's not associate impermanence only with the negative. Without anicca the foolish could never become wise, the ill could never become well, and the poor could never even dream of riches. Over time, change offers happiness and unhappiness, joy and sorrow. That is the nature of things.

We can refuse to accept change and spend a great deal of time and money trying to disguise it, but it is a battle we cannot win. So why not stay as healthy as you can, age gracefully, and be patient with the body? Aging, illness, and death are as natural as birth. You are not being punished, you've done nothing wrong. The great baseball player Mickey Mantle said, "If I knew I was going to live this long I'd have taken better care of myself." That's worth considering.

As we become aware of the body aging we need to accept and adjust patiently and gracefully. Remember, with age we have also gained experience. Perhaps we have even grown a bit wiser.

> When I start to become impatient I stop and ask myself, "How important is this in the light of all eternity?"
>
> —A Catholic nun

Unsatisfactoriness

In the context of the three characteristics we can think of the term *dukkha* as meaning unsatisfactoriness. Thus, one of the characteristics of all phenomena is that they are unsatisfactory. If you ever wondered why Buddhism is viewed by some as pessimistic this may be the reason. But the Buddha simply saw that dukkha was the basic problem with which we all have to live, and based on his own experience he offered a remedy. He was like a doctor diagnosing a disease and then offering a cure. Pessimism would have been to walk away saying there is an illness and no cure. He saw the opposite: that sustainable happiness was possible and could come about through our own efforts. While other traditions suggest that after the struggles of this life there is the hope of peace and happiness in some type of paradise, the Buddha offered a path to peace and joy in this very life. When we see things as they really are, we can free ourselves from the delusions that lead to sorrow and experience the real joys and delights of each precious moment of this life right now.

What causes the illness, said the Buddha, is endless craving/clinging/desire. We crave things—power, money, sex, fame—believing, on some level, that they will bring us happiness. There is nothing wrong with having things and enjoying beautiful experiences. It is when we cling to them, endlessly craving more, believing that our happiness is derived from phenomena outside ourselves, that we will be disappointed and experience dukkha. Things can bring pleasant feelings, but because of their impermanent nature those feelings cannot last. So we crave more experiences and more things and the pursuit of happiness goes on and on. We cling to things, people, and events, desiring each moment of pleasure to continue. We move faster and faster, trying to piece together moments of happiness so that the characteristic of unsatisfactoriness is unfelt. It is an exhausting endeavor in which we lose because even if we could keep up the pace, things outside of ourselves cannot bring inner peace and lasting happiness.

The Buddha offers another way. It doesn't speak of pursuing happiness, but instead of bringing about the cessation of unhappiness (dukkha). The Four Noble Truths teach (1) there is dukkha; we all know empirically about stress, disappointment, suffering, discomfort, and anxiety; (2) when we stop and examine carefully we can see that there is a cause of dukkha; (3) accordingly, to bring about the end of dukkha, we must stop creating the cause; (4) the Noble Eightfold Path[3] lays out a way of living that leads to the end of dukkha.

We cannot throw dukkha away or bury it. So what then? Let us use fire again as an example. To extinguish a fire we don't throw water on the flames, we throw water on what is burning. Fire exists because a fuel (wood, paper) has been heated to a point where it becomes combustible. To put out the fire we must cool the fuel so that it can no longer burn. The same is true in extinguishing dukkha. We cool the fuel, which, in the case of dukkha, is the causes and conditions that bring about suffering. In other words, we do what is necessary to change that which causes dukkha. Thus, we stop bringing about our unhappiness. Correspondingly, we encourage within ourselves more skillful and more wholesome thoughts, words, and actions. This advances us on the path to inner peace and happiness. Greater patience is a natural outgrowth.

> If I need proof that it is me myself who causes me to feel impatient, not the other person, it's the phases I go through. On a

---

3. Skillful view, skillful intention, skillful speech, skillful action, skillful livelihood, skillful effort, skillful mindfulness, and skillful concentration.

day when I am feeling calm and peaceful, very little triggers my impatience, but when I'm irritated and cranky, look out, world.

—AN OHIO MINISTER

Not-Self

As we consider ways to develop patience with ourselves, it can be beneficial to look at the Buddhist teaching of anatta, or "not-self."[4] The concept of anatta can be challenging simply because it is not the way we usually think, and conditioned thinking so readily holds sway. Nevertheless, the anatta doctrine offers potential for freedom from constrictive views, and that makes a brief exploration warranted. This may also present an opportunity to observe how receptive we may or may not be to thinking that is different from our own. An open "beginner's mind" is a powerful tool for developing patience. Notice if you tend to be curious and remain open-minded about thoughts that are different or in opposition to your current views, or do you quickly reject that which doesn't come easily or immediately seem "right"? Recognizing that we resist the new and different can reveal insights about our issues with patience.

As to the not-self concept, let's start by acknowledging that there is a self—it just isn't the self we usually think of as self. You really are there, holding a book or an e-reader. There is a body

4. Found in the *Anatta Lakkhana* Sutra in the Samyutta Nikaya ("Connected Discourses") of the Pali Canon.

and there is the experience of sensation. There is also the experience of thoughts, feelings, and emotions. But the teaching of anatta says there is no possessor of those thoughts, feelings, and emotions; they are not happening to a fixed, unchanging self. There is only the experience. It is as if to say there are thoughts but not a thinker, feelings but not a feeler, emotions but not an emoter. Thoughts, feelings, and sensations arise and die away in a continuous flow, but they are not happening to a self. Now, 2,500 years after the Buddha offered this view, scientists have conducted tests using neuroimaging that look specifically for something inside us that could be identified as the *self*, the *black box*, the actual *Allan/Sara/Thomas*, but no such self has been found.

The Buddha was not rejecting the conventional, convenient designation *I*. These types of labels are necessary if we are to communicate in a stable society. He was disputing the misperception of *I* as representing a fixed, solid, and immutable entity. He posited that the human being is an assemblage of parts which he referred to as *aggregates*.[5] To illustrate the point he spoke of *chariot* as being a name for an assemblage of parts. The wheels are not the chariot nor are the spokes of the wheels. The rails are not the chariot nor is the cart. All the parts are necessary for there to be a chariot. However, there is no chariot apart from the assemblage of parts. When the parts are separated there is no chariot. Or we can take apart a flower, removing its petals, leaves, stamen,

5. Buddhism views the human being as being comprised of five aggregates: form (material, physical), feeling (pleasant, unpleasant, or neutral), perception (the formation of a conception regarding a particular phenomenon), mental formations (a conditioned response to the object of experience), and consciousness (the presence of which produces experience).

and stem. See how the flower is comprised only of its component parts? There is no self. The terminology used is that it is *empty* of a self. The notion of self is therefore said to be an illusion.

The Buddha's interest was in helping us to end our suffering, and, accordingly, when asked specifically if there was a self he did not answer. It is likely that he did not want us distracted by pursuing matters that did not directly relate to the end of dukkha. (Or perhaps he sensed that just trying to comprehend the concept of not-self could itself be a cause for a certain amount of dukkha.) Yet to open the door and take a peek at the possibility that the self as we tend to understand it may not be entirely accurate can be of benefit to us. The ramifications associated with *I*, *me*, and *mine*, the clinging, the concerns, and the anxieties, might no longer have to be suffered and defended. We could experience the words and deeds of others with greater ease and patience. We might even be more patient with our (non)selves. What is important at this juncture is not whether we believe in a "self" in the conventional way, but whether we can learn to relinquish our views long enough to listen patiently to others. If so, we will have taken a major step toward peaceful living.

A friend once said, "I think I have a pretty good understanding of anatta. Nevertheless, if there is no self, whose back is it that's killing me?"

Profile in Patience: Michael Naranjo

Not long ago I was teaching in the Southwest and on a day off in Albuquerque I found myself in a shop that specialized in fine Native American art. As I was admiring a particularly beautiful ceramic pot a man walked over and told me that the pot was indeed rare and extraordinary. I soon learned that he was an American history scholar with a wealth of knowledge about Native American art. We continued chatting, and before long he and his wife invited Susanna and me to their home/gallery in Santa Fe. We accepted the invitation, and were amazed at the enormous collection they had amassed through the years. It was there that I first saw the work of Michael Naranjo, a Native American sculptor who, in the Vietnam War, had been blinded and had his right hand seriously injured. In spite of the challenges with which he worked, Michael had become one of America's most renowned sculptors. His work now appears in major museums and important collections throughout the world including the Vatican, the White House, and the Heard Museum in Phoenix, Arizona.

Early the next morning I awoke with the compelling feeling that Michael Naranjo would have insights into the virtue of patience that I couldn't possibly have and I should make every effort to meet him. I called the gallery that represented him, introduced myself, and requested that they ask Michael if he would be willing to meet with me. Less than five minutes later my phone rang and Michael's gentle voice, sounding like that of an old friend, extended an invitation to come to his home outside Santa Fe. I loaded an application into my iPad so that I could record our conversation, and the next day Susanna and I got in our car and headed south. About an hour later we arrived at our destination and were greeted by a shy man of average height with silver hair, who extended his left hand for a handshake. A moment later Michael's wife, Laurie, appeared, an attractive non–Native American, who is from Westchester County in New York. They had been married for thirty-two years, and while Michael had never actually seen Laurie or their two daughters, it was soon evident that they had forged a deep, loving, and supportive relationship. My instinct was right; these two people had indeed learned a great deal about patience.

Michael was born in Santa Fe in 1944 and grew up in the Santa Clara Pueblo. His early life on the reservation influenced his work as did the many stories he heard from the elders. He said, "I sculpt from my memories of the birds and the animals since I can no longer see them. I remember as a boy sitting on top of the peaks above the timberline, and just sitting there with my brother. It was a happy time. We didn't talk very much. We might just watch a bird or a cloud slowly coming towards the mountain and feathering out, floating over us, over the ridge, and onto wherever it was going."

I was curious about how Michael had felt when he received notice that he had to serve in the military of a country that had historically treated his people poorly, without honor. "I don't really remember how I felt except that I knew I had to go. In basic training they showed us a film about the U.S. Army and what they had accomplished. In one of the scenes they showed a fight going on with Indians and I didn't like it. I was disturbed by it because of the way the native people in this country were treated and moved around. I guess I felt frustration and some anger. I didn't enjoy the army but I think I was a good soldier."

Michael was only in Vietnam for six weeks, but even in that short time he felt he had grown immune to emotions because he had become somewhat dead. "In order to survive you had to remove yourself emotionally. If you didn't you would go crazy. I think that's why a lot of young men come back the way they do. First dead person I saw I thought I was going to get sick. I had to walk away. Somehow it changes you." He described being in basic training, and looking at his group, his fellow young recruits. There was an innocence about them, an innocence their two instructors seemed to have lost. He couldn't quite find the words for it; perhaps the instructors just looked hardened. "I know the day that it happened to me," he said. "I walked into a thatched hut when we went looking for Vietcong and there was an old Vietnamese man sitting there at a table. He smiled and he poured a cup of tea. He picked it up and gestured, offering it to me. I'm standing there with my M16 pointing at him. Imagine, I'm there with an M16 pointing at him and he offered me tea, smiling at me. I looked at him and motioned "you drink," and he drank the tea. He poured another cup and offered it to me, and I looked at him and shook my head no, and turned and walked away. I thought, *My goodness, what has happened to me? How could I do that to another human being?* At that moment I realized I had changed."

Michael told me he was open to speaking about any of his experiences so I worked my way around to the day he was injured.

He seemed calm and focused as he recalled in great detail what had occurred more than forty years earlier:

> That morning was very tense. I came around a leg with my squad and all of a sudden lots of shots rang out. I looked across and I saw Morgan fall like a wet cloth, and the man behind him, Black, fell, and then everyone hit the dirt. Then there was silence. When I hit the dirt I laid there for two or three seconds. Then I jumped up and charged straight ahead and then shots rang out and I knew they were meant for me. The minute I heard the first shot I hit the dirt and then the shots stopped. I charged again, and again more shots. Then I advanced again. Then Stuart and Young got shot and they were dead. Then Doc was killed. I crawled up another several yards, right up to the corner of the dike where it met at the top of a T. I was looking over right into where they were in front of me, but I couldn't see them. It was jungle there. Apparently they had been in there for a while—how long I don't know. Then I went crawling around the edge of a dike and on the other side was a little mud depression where I guess water had collected. It was muddy and when I looked over I saw this Vietcong out of a foxhole with palm leaves draped over him looking for someone else to shoot. I pointed my rifle at him and he suddenly turned and we looked at each other. I shot and he fell.
>
> I couldn't bring my rifle down with me into the mud so I had it right along the edge of a depression. I rolled over slightly on my right side and then I saw this round ball roll past me. I knew immediately what it was. I turned toward it but I couldn't see it again. Then there was an explosion, and then there was

silence, then a hum and I knew I was going to die. My thoughts were, *Dear God, don't make it too hard on my parents.* Then I waited to die. But instead I heard Yazir's voice say, "Baby, are you okay?" and I realized I was still alive, so I said, "Just get me out of here." I asked him how bad it was, and he said, "You're okay." I must have been bleeding everywhere and I didn't know about my eyes. At that point I couldn't see, but I didn't feel pain. It didn't hurt, really, but slowly it started to throb.

Then there was a chaplain and he asked me if I believed in God. I said, "Yeah," because in those days I did. I have different beliefs now. I guess he was giving me last rites. I don't know. It started to hurt then and I told them I couldn't see. Someone had called medevac already. They flung me up into the chopper and it took off. I kept talking because I knew that if I stopped talking I would die.

At that time Michael didn't know anything about the extent of his injuries and several times he said that more than anything he was grateful he was alive. Later, in a hospital, he received over a hundred stitches, but he kept reminding himself that he was alive and he was able to think. He felt that as long as his mind was clear he would be okay. He learned that his right hand was badly damaged and that he had lost the use of one eye. He was moved to a hospital in Japan, where they tried to save the other eye, but those efforts failed and he was blind.

"In that hospital, straight across from me was this man who couldn't hear anymore. He cried a lot. There's always someone who is worse off. Men would come in sometimes very angry and bitter and find themselves next to someone with one arm and no legs, and in a matter of twenty-four hours their attitude changed. I was angry too. A nurse took me for a walk one day and I remember this fly buzzing around me and I thought, *That fly can see but I can't.* I guess I was angry for a while, but what was I going to do? The fact of being alive and having my mind was much better than being dead."

Before coming home Michael was in a hospital in DC. They had done extensive skin grafting on his arm and he couldn't get out of bed. When a volunteer asked if he wanted anything, Michael asked for some clay.

> So now on my bed tray there was a block of clay that I could touch with my left hand. I left it sitting there for a long time because by now I knew I wanted to be a sculptor and I was afraid if I couldn't make anything then my dream would be gone.
>
> I finally tore off a piece of clay the size of a golf ball and rolled it out and made a string, put a squiggle in it, wiggled this way and that, made a little head, two little eyes, a little mouth with my fingernail, and put lines around its body. At that moment I knew I could sculpt. I had made a little worm. Then with the next piece of clay I made a goldfish. Then I made a crude figure of a thinker, and with the last little bit of clay I made a squirrel with a nut in its hand. I was ecstatic. I knew what I was going to do with my life.

Even though he couldn't see and had very little use of his right hand, Michael knew he would be a sculptor. As Beethoven didn't need to hear to write music, Michael didn't need to see to sculpt.

Michael was then moved to a hospital in Denver, where a remarkable event occurred. While in his bed he made a clay Indian on a horse. Someone took a picture of it and it got into a newspaper. Actually, it made the front pages of newspapers all across the country. Letters began pouring in from people saying that if Michael made another one, they wanted to buy it. In spite of all the praise, Michael destroyed the piece and made something else, a bear with a fish in its mouth. Michael's highly perfectionistic nature was becoming evident.

The next hospital was the Western Blind Rehabilitation Center in Palo Alto, California, where he learned to read Braille and to use a cane, a skill he found easy enough, but scary.

> It was like being born again. I wasn't sick, I was just blind and I had one good hand. That was all that was wrong. I could still do things. My instructor taught me how to cross a street. Wait for the traffic to go, then take your time. The first time I tried, the light changed three times before I crossed the street because I didn't know what would happen if I went off at an angle or hit the corner on the other side. I wasn't being patient, I was just scared. I remembered when I could see, sometimes I saw a little frog that had been run over and it was flat like a silhouette. I knew that's what I could look like in the next few seconds. But once I took that first step and went across, tap tap with my cane, and I reached the other side, then everything was okay.

Some of Michael's favorite pieces that were never offered for sale grace his home. I wondered if it was frustrating for him to have never seen his own work. He acknowledged that sometimes it was, but his frustration seemed to be more about when a piece was not coming along the way he wanted. "Once there was a war dancer I was making and it just didn't work so I left it and made something else. I've learned to be patient. Six months later I came back and picked it up and then the time was right; then it worked. When it's not working, I know it's not working and I must be patient. If it's going to happen it will happen, but if I can't do it, then I can't do it."

For the last several years Michael has dealt with severe headaches stemming from an acute spinal condition. Surgery has not helped and his patience can be tried when the pain is at its worst. The combination of pain, which Michael describes as beyond what one could imagine, plus not being able to see, causes him at times to experience memory failure and a loss of equanimity. It is Laurie's kind, sweet, caring nature that gets him through. It is her gentleness, honesty, and intelligence that originally attracted Michael to the woman he has never seen. For Laurie, it was Michael's courage, honesty, and inner strength. I was curious about how they dealt with impatience when it would arise between them. Michael said that he is not a particularly verbal person, but Laurie had a way of getting him to speak about what might be bothering him. "One day I woke up grumpy. Anyone on a given day can be grumpy. She took my hand, walked me back into the bedroom, and said, 'Get into bed and then get out on the other side.' I did, and then we were laughing. That's how she deals with me." When Laurie gets impatient with Michael she will sometimes process it within herself, but she has found that eventually she will have to talk about it. "If I don't," she said, "it feels tight. It just doesn't feel good. Of course, I have to find the right time and place and then, when we talk about it, we both feel better."

I went back to something he had said about his spiritual beliefs having changed, and he explained it this way:

> I no longer believe in organized religion. I believe in you and Susanna and Laurie and me, the good in us. No one is perfect, but we try, and we try to make as few mistakes as possible and learn from yesterday. We're not always so good at it. Man is made so that he just can't seem to get it right all the time even with a second chance. We're spirit as we are, here and now, this bundle of energy. What we do with it is what we get out of life. How we affect the world around us; we make choices and we live by those choices and that's all we can do. I don't know if there is anything after this life and it doesn't matter because there's nothing you can do about it. So you do what you think is right and love those around you. Find peace within yourself because that makes you happy. I say these things, but it's not always so easy to live by. But I try.

Michael had recently received a lifetime achievement award from the Southwestern Association for Indian Arts and I was curious to know how he felt about his life, a life that had known incredibly difficult times as well as recognition and honor as one of the great sculptors of his time. So I asked if he felt it had been a good life. He answered without hesitation: "I wouldn't trade shoes with any man. I like the soles of my feet—they're mine."

As Susanna and I drove back to town we were silent, which is unusual for us since we like to discuss our experiences. It reminded me of a time many years ago when I went to Carnegie Hall to hear the great German baritone Dietrich Fischer-Dieskau sing Schubert's *Die Winterreise.* I sat in the last row of the balcony, and when the concert ended I walked down the winding flights of marble stairs with hundreds of others, and it was absolutely silent. Or of when we were gorilla trekking in Rwanda and a female gorilla sat down next to me and held my arm. There are those rare experiences that reach so far down into our being that no words can find their way out of the chasm. All we can do is breathe and wipe away the tears.

I think about Michael Naranjo's Native American upbringing and the long days in the mountains and plains with his brother, how as boys they took in the world in silence. How did that peace and quiet contribute to the man who has been through hell and who now, with patience and determination, has reached a place where he "wouldn't trade shoes with any man"?

CONTEMPLATIONS

Looking after oneself, one is looking after others. Looking after others, one is looking after oneself. How does one accomplish this looking after others by looking after oneself? By practicing and developing mindfulness, thus encouraging it to grow. How does one accomplish this looking after oneself by looking after others? By practicing patience, compassion, and lovingkindness.

—Buddha, Samyutta Nikaya 47:19

I know not of anything that brings such happiness as the mind that has been brought under control, is well attended and restrained. Such a mind does indeed yield great happiness.

—Buddha, Anguttara Nikaya 1:3–4

Practice

Happiness, inner peace, and patience begin with taming the mind. The mind's incessant tendency to jump from thought to thought, feeling to feeling, can be brought under control. We do not have to be governed by the mind's random nature. Make the practice of mindfulness the ground upon which you will build greater patience and inner peace. Commit to taking time each day to sit down, even for a few minutes, to practice detailed awareness of the workings of your mind. Just be aware, don't judge. It is a sophisticated skill and takes time to learn, but even your initial efforts can yield benefits. Let go of thoughts that will lead to dukkha and welcome thoughts that will lead to happiness. While ultimately patience is practiced in the company of others, the starting place is in your own mind.

Part 2

With a little experience you will also be able to recognize physical sensations as they arise in the body. Sit quietly and bring your awareness to those sensations and, again, just observe. Be in touch with the bare experience, nothing else. Notice its changing nature. You may discover that certain sensations arise when you feel agitated or annoyed. As you become familiar with those sensations they can serve as signals that alert you to when you are becoming impatient in a real-life situation. Then you can pause and rationally decide how best to respond. You are much more likely to act with greater wisdom and dignity.

Relationships

> One day, Ananda,[1] who had been deep in thought for a while, addressed the Buddha saying, "I've been thinking, spiritual friendship seems at least half of the spiritual life." The Buddha replied, "Not so, Ananda, not so. Spiritual friendship comprises the entire spiritual life."
>
> —BUDDHA, SAMYUTTA NIKAYA 3:18

Every moment of our lives is spent in relationship with someone or something and every relationship has the potential to bring about both joy and sorrow. As noted previously, we are always in a relationship with self, which becomes abundantly clear when we spend quiet time with ourselves such as in meditation practice. There we can see whether we treat ourselves honorably with kindness and compassion or are overly self-critical and easily annoyed. Do we allow the spaciousness in which we can forgive our unskillful actions and do we have a genuine interest in learning from our mistakes, or are we unforgiving and harshly critical of our imperfections? Are we patient with

1. The Buddha's attendant.

ourselves? If not, can we really expect to be kind and patient with others?

This type of self-examination is essential if we want to bring greater joy and reverence to our relationships. Although the boss or the noisy neighbor can often try our patience, it is our relationships with those we care about most that can, at times, present the most challenging issues, undoubtedly for the very reason that these are the relationships that matter most to us. This is where we are emotionally most heavily invested. Our long history with a parent, brother, sister, or other relative can be laden with offenses and misunderstandings. Our relationship with a significant other can be easily stressed as together we maneuver the choppy waters of the ocean of our days. This is the person with whom we make the decisions that determine the course of our lives.

Intimacy

The Bible uses the phrase "He knew her" to describe sexual relations between two people. Since translators had so many terms they could have used that would have been inoffensive to most people it is interesting to consider why they chose these particular words. One view might be that sexual intimacy is the closest one human being can come to actually knowing another. Two people open up to each other in a way that reveals more of themselves physically, mentally, and emotionally than in any other of life's experiences. In this joyful giving of self, in this passionate loving of each other, we willingly allow ourselves to be most vulnerable. When this union exists between two people who have entered into a monogamous relationship it is reverential and an expression of the deepest trust one being can have in another. Therefore, if we dishonor that trust and betray our partner there will likely be enormous suffering. Rage, betrayal, confusion, sadness, and a loss of self-esteem that is felt throughout one's entire being can all be experienced by the betrayed partner. The rebuilding of trust can be a long and challenging process and is not always successful no matter how much a couple may want it to happen. Unfortunately, it's difficult to enjoy the company of someone who has been untruthful or unfaithful.

My student Arthur lived with his fiancée, Josie. One day Arthur came home and found Josie on their bed locked in an embrace with her acting coach, Jason. Her blouse was unbuttoned as were his trousers. At the sight of Arthur, Jason was out the door quickly and Josie was silent. Arthur confronted her and became more and more incensed by what he felt were her ludicrous responses. As he stormed out of the apartment Josie grabbed his arm, but Arthur shoved her away with considerable force and Josie was thrown to the floor. Arthur glanced down and saw she was all right and left. He went back a few days later to pack up his things and never returned. He had loved Josie and assumed they would spend the rest of their lives together, but her betrayal and seemingly inane explanations left Arthur brokenhearted. Over the next several years Arthur was in a few short relationships and then met Caroline. They fell in love, got married, and now have a son who is a scholar-in-the-making and a star on his elementary school softball team.

When Arthur thinks back to that day with Josie, what causes him the most distress is the moment when he lost control and shoved her to the floor. He has long since forgiven her. They were young; she was sweet; she made a mistake. But his one reactive moment, that loss of composure, justified though he may have felt it was, could have been disastrous. Prisons are filled with people whose lives were changed in an instant when they lost control and committed a "crime of passion."

My father was institutionalized a number of times for a serious mental condition. When I would visit him we would meet in a large community-type room designated for visitations. The room had perhaps twenty card tables, usually with two, three, or four people sitting at each and chatting. Sometimes I would look around the room and try to figure out which ones were the patients and which ones were the visitors. Everyone was dressed in street clothes and no one was jumping up and down or howling like a wolf or attempting to strangle someone. I never could figure out which ones were the patients.

Gail was attractive, bright, and articulate. There was nothing to indicate that she was any different in nature from the scores of folks we have all met throughout our lives. Indeed, she was probably not all that much different from any of the people with whom we live, work, and socialize every day, except for the fact that when she was thirty years old she had killed her husband.

It would be seriously naive to think that what toppled her life and caused the death of another could never happen to you or me. If there were any such naïveté on my part it was quickly obliterated when I heard how easily a disagreement could become a disaster. It seems her husband, while mostly loving and thoughtful, could also be harsh and critical. She felt he was never quite satisfied with her as a partner. One day she told him that she wanted to talk about starting a family. His response was that they shouldn't rush into it. He didn't think she was ready to be a parent. She felt a cold shiver go through her body and she lashed out at him verbally, which she had never done before. He called her outburst a perfect example of her immaturity. Things quickly escalated. He grabbed her wrists, insisting that she was being ridiculous and should grow up. They were both shouting as she pulled away and he grabbed at her again. She swung at him, almost unaware that she now had a heavy vase in her hand. He fell to the floor and was pronounced dead that evening. She was convicted of manslaughter and died in prison three years later.

The second step of the Buddhist Noble Eightfold Path is *samma sankappa,* which means "right thinking."[2] To think *I could never, ever do such a thing* would be an example of *wrong* thinking. That is not to say you are likely to commit a violent crime, but the *never* part is what is questionable. Every action arises out of causes and conditions and, as we have seen, everything is constantly changing, moment by moment. When we think of ourselves in fixed, nonmalleable terms such as *always* or *never,* we are not seeing into the nature of reality.

When a person with no history of violence commits a violent crime we often learn afterward that the person may have been

2. Sometimes translated as "right intention" or "right aspiration."

suppressing feelings of anger, fear, or frustration for a long time, perhaps since early childhood. They may have often seemed impatient or annoyed and those around them just assumed that was "the way they were." Sometimes we ourselves might wish we were more patient, but we don't really have the time to do anything about it. It would be unreasonable to suggest that anyone who is more impatient than the norm (however that would be measured) is a ticking time bomb. Impatience, anger, and fear are all natural feelings. It is how we relate to our feelings and how we respond to them that is so important.

We want to strive for a more awakened way of life. Often a major event such as a life-threatening illness or the loss of a loved one opens the door to greater awakening. Such life-altering events, which can motivate positive action, are often accompanied by thoughts like, *Why did I need this frightening experience to get me to wake up? What can I learn from this? What should I do now?* These are significant questions and we would do well to sit with them and contemplate. What are you doing that is so important that you can't devote a few minutes each day to developing greater self-awareness?

In the Native American Apache tradition, when two people commit themselves to a monogamous relationship this blessing is frequently offered:

> Now you will feel no rain, for each of you will be shelter to the other. Now you will feel no cold, for each of you will be warmth to the other. Now there is no loneliness for you, for each of you

will be a companion to the other. You are two persons, but there is only one life before you. Go now to your dwelling place to enter into your days together, and may your days be good and long upon the earth.

The trust and responsibility of a sacred union is felt in these words. The commitment that two independent beings make to share a life together, and perhaps to bring new life into the world, is sacred and not to be taken lightly. The development of patience by both partners with each other can provide the glue that holds things together during life's stressful times.

If we want others to listen to our views, we must be willing to listen to theirs. When it comes to political and religious discussions, even with our most dearly loved ones, we should know in advance that disagreement can be lurking behind the next apostrophe. This is when we want to listen respectfully and with regard for the feelings of the other. No matter how far afield the views of another may be from our own, rest assured that it is safe to listen. If your views tend to be liberal, you won't become infected by a conservative opinion, and vice versa. For instance, the sluggishness of our governments to grant equal rights to all citizens, including same-sex couples, is disturbing to many and tries the patience of otherwise unruffled beings. Those who find the legal sale of guns to be unacceptable cringe every time a law makes it even easier for someone to buy a dangerous weapon. These are topics about which many hold strong views. If we choose to discuss such subjects it is the perfect time to practice the admirable skill of patient listening. As an exercise, you can check to see if you heard the other person accurately, or were you influenced by the agree/disagree dialogue going on in your head? Quickly formed opinions may be hindrances to patience. We can become so convinced of the validity of our views that we can't hear those of the other. You can be sure that will try the patience of others just as it does yours. You might instead say to the other, "So, did I hear you say . . . ?" Say what you heard and ask for confirmation that you heard correctly. Try to repeat the words you heard and not your interpretation.

Watch carefully what goes on in your mind as you listen to views that are in opposition to your own. Those thoughts and feelings may also be detected as sensations in the body. Become familiar with those sensations. They might be indicating reactive or conditioned responses or a lack of openness to the views of others. In the quiet of meditation we have an excellent opportunity to observe the relationship between thoughts and feelings and their subsequent physical sensations. (Look again at the practices at the end of the previous chapter.)

The Buddha observed that all phenomena, including thoughts, feelings, and perceptions, have three characteristics: anicca (impermanence), dukkha (unsatisfactoriness), and anatta (not-self). Phenomena arise and die away constantly, according to a complex matrix of causes and conditions. When we see this truth in relation to our impatience, we can become more willing to release views to which we may have been clinging for years. Even absolute, unquestionable fact has been known to become more obsolete than absolute. When in disagreement it is simply wiser to listen with the grace of patience and use your intelligence to work out acceptable solutions.

When we live under the same roof with another all the rough edges and unfinished corners that are part of our humanness become revealed. There are an infinite number of reasons why we might become impatient with our partner/wife/husband, but when it comes to what matters most, we all want the same thing. All sentient beings want to be happy; no one wants to suffer. Notwithstanding that, we each experience life from an individual perspective, with our own thoughts, feelings, and sensations continually arising and fading away. One partner may squeeze the toothpaste tube from the top while the other leaves the bed unmade; one rolls up yesterday's clothes and tosses them in a corner and the other leaves the dirty dishes in the sink; he forgets to take out the garbage and she doesn't close the garage door, and on and on. Each of these (in)actions can be a source of annoyance for the other partner and, since they may have asked many times that one or more of the above (not) be done, these can become the cause of irritation and subsequent loss of patience.

While some of the activities above may seem trivial they can grow into issues for conflict when one party feels they have patiently asked many times that they be done differently. The issue can then become about a sense of not being heard or feelings not being honored. If the other partner, perhaps feeling defensive, then retaliates and points out how their requests have also not been met, the heat gets turned up. Patience wears thin and a mountain grows from what could have been a simple molehill. It is usually best to address issues before they get out of hand.

Then there are the bigger questions that many couples have to answer, such as where they will live, will they have children, how shall finances be handled, and so forth. Over time, most of us come to realize that to be in a joyful and meaningful relationship, particularly an intimate one, we must learn to speak skillfully, listen attentively, and practice patience. Things will not always be the way we want them to be or the way we think they should be. We must learn to listen objectively not only to the words of our partner, but also to the underlying messages as well. Watch their expression; open your heart, especially when you are disagreeing. Remember that the person with whom you are angry is also the person you love.

The first step to becoming a skillful listener is remembering that you care about the other. You may have to negotiate and you want to do so fairly. If you are always winning the chances are you are losing. Listen, listen, listen. Don't keep explaining why you are right and expect your loved one to remain patient. Just like you, they want a fair chance. Think of their happiness and you will be more patient. Think of their happiness and *you* will be happier. Life is amazing, mysterious, miraculous, and extraordinarily complex. Joining two lives together can enhance the joys and multiply the complexities. Being part of a meaningful relationship is an ongoing, and at times, challenging adventure.

We all have issues and we have usually come by them honestly. If we have a fear of dogs, for instance, chances are we were frightened in some way by a dog when we were young, or perhaps a parent had a fear of dogs and transferred it to us. It is unlikely that we just make up a fear without some related background, subtle though it may be. When two people are in an intimate relationship it is important that both have a good sense of their own issues so that they don't act in a reactive or accusative way when something triggers uncomfortable feelings. As an example, if we deal regularly with feelings of jealousy, we want to be aware of that so we don't start making accusations or snide comments about a situation that might not actually exist. If both partners are well familiar with their own individual issues it is easier to see the issues they have as a couple. Therefore, understand that there are *my* issues, *your* issues, and *our* issues. When both parties take the time to patiently learn which is which, they can avoid a great deal of dukkha.

The *Brahma Viharas,*[3] also referred to as the Four Immeasurables, are four mental states, or virtues, that are practiced in Buddhist meditation and carried out in one's daily activities. They are said to establish an ideal mental, emotional, and intellectual environment for spiritual growth. These qualities are *metta* (lovingkindness), *karuna* (compassion), *mudita* (altruistic joy), and *upekkha* (equanimity). The nonmeditator can find these four practices of great benefit as well. For example, when disagreement begins to arise we can shift our aggressive, fearful mind to offer the other person metta, silent friendly thoughts such as *May you be happy and free from suffering*. If you're thinking it might be difficult to do that, especially if you are feeling annoyed, perhaps so. That's why it's called a "practice." We have to practice a practice if it is to be of value. Imagine, however, having at your disposal a

3. Sanskrit and Pali: "Heavenly Abodes."

skill to defuse your anger before you lash out with a conditioned response or a knee-jerk reaction; the kind of reaction we usually regret later, the kind that can damage a treasured relationship. As we practice metta we may find ourselves more present, more gentle, and more caring. With the practice of metta we are also developing patience. As patience grows deeper it becomes a characteristic of who we are. Our thoughts, words, and actions reflect more of the person we want to be.

By practicing karuna, compassion for ourselves and for all beings, our heart becomes more spacious, more willing to accept, more able to feel the distress of others. Compassion can be thought of as the quivering of the heart in relation to the suffering of another. When we see that others feel stress, concern, and anxiety as we do, we can allow ourselves to soften, to be more patient and caring. We realize that being right isn't as important as being happy and caring about the happiness of others. One student told me that he was afraid if he were open and kind in this way others would take advantage of him. I asked how it felt to be guarded and closed off and he acknowledged that it didn't feel very good. He often felt a tightness in the center of his chest. I suggested that he gradually try the practice of karuna starting with those he felt he could trust and then slowly see how it felt opening to others. So far he has reported that people have responded warmly to his more open self and he finds himself to be noticeably less stressed.

Mudita can be the most challenging of the Brahma Viharas. Altruistic joy (or, my preferred translation, harmonious joy) invites us to be genuinely happy for the good fortune of all beings. There is a logic to this practice. If I am happy when something good happens for me, that's wonderful. If I can also be happy for the good fortune of someone close to me, then I have doubled my opportunities to be happy. If I likewise am joyful for the good fortune of twenty friends and acquaintances, then I have multiplied my chances to be happy by twentyfold. So we expand this view outward and ultimately share in the joy and good fortune of all beings. The operative word that makes this practice challenging is the *all* in *all beings*. In fact, it is the challenge throughout the Brahma Viharas. When we practice metta we wish for *all* beings to be happy, free from suffering. Likewise, karuna practice opens our compassionate heart to *all* beings. That, as you can imagine, is not always easy, and the best approach, again, is to go slowly, without self-judgment or criticism.

As we consider our personal relationships we want to be aware of any competitive or conflicted feelings we might have for those with whom we are closest. If our loved one receives a great promotion with a substantial increase in pay, or is publicly recognized for professional excellence, can we be unboundedly delighted for them? If not, and it's good to look deeply to be sure, we might be harboring a bit of resentment that could later cause an angry eruption over a seemingly unrelated matter. It is difficult to practice patience when we don't see things as they really are. Looking directly at issues and acknowledging them can help dispel their detrimental power. This is particularly important when it involves little unspoken grievances we may be harboring toward a loved one.

Sometimes I think of upekkha as one of the great rewards we derive from traversing the spiritual path. Equanimity is the ability to remain calm, emotionally balanced, and impartial amidst the turbulence of life's ever-changing nature. Impermanence, the realization that there is nothing to grasp on to that is permanent and unchanging, can be a great source of dukkha. Equanimity enables us to move gently and patiently *with* change rather than feeling we are in conflict with the natural ways of the universe.

When I teach the Brahma Viharas I always advise people to go slowly and to be gentle with themselves. Spiritual practice in any tradition is not easy. We live in a world where kindness is almost viewed as a secondary quality, not as respected as aggression, ambition, or toughness. I have heard members of my own family say that in their office they would rather be feared than liked. As a society we seem to enjoy posturing and claiming that we are "number one." I assume that is supposed to be significant, although I'm not sure why. Such attitudes in the home will surely try the patience of our loved ones. The Brahma Viharas, kindness, compassion, joy, and equanimity, can be the building blocks for inner peace and meaningful relationships. With patience we can develop deeper levels of these virtuous qualities.

> When I can't identify with someone's idiotic behavior as something I would do, I admit to myself that I must behave in ways that appear as idiotic to others. I'm just not aware of it.
>
> —A PHYSICAL FITNESS TRAINER

Children

Two dear friends have a pillow in their home embroidered with the words *Insanity is inherited—you get it from your children.*

My eleven-year-old friend, Charlene, is bright, precocious, and utterly irresistible. She adores her mother and clearly the feeling is mutual. One day I met them in the street and as I approached, Charlene pointed to her mom and said, "She's annoying." She had a saucy look of childlike frustration on her face so I resisted smiling and responded to her comment seriously. "Of course she's annoying," I answered, "that's part of her job. Sometimes parents have to be annoying." With a look of resignation, Charlene answered simply, "Oh."

If only it were always that easy. Few would argue that the job of parenting is one of the most challenging, if not *the* most challenging a human being can undertake. There are, of course, exceptions, but by and large parenting will challenge one's physical, mental, and emotional resources like no other endeavor. When it comes to patience, parenting will likely offer an unparalleled opportunity to practice again and again. In the early weeks of life with a new arrival, one may search for previously unused adjectives to describe a depth of fatigue hitherto unimagined. Yet for most of us, more often than not, the frustration, turmoil, and exhaustion are worth it because the joys outweigh the difficulties. Just when we think we cannot get through another moment, the infant offers her first smile. When it seems that having this baby was the biggest mistake you've ever made, he looks at you and utters, "Mama." The precious, indescribable moments that begin from the newborn's earliest days can bring incomparable joy, or at least enough pleasure that we resist offering them on eBay when our patience becomes shredded.

You survive their "terrible twos" and make it to their teens when all you have to contend with is drugs, alcohol, and sex. They finish their schooling and you're almost there; you've almost completed the task. Then you learn, perhaps dramatically, that *you never complete the task*; you are a parent, period, till death do you part, and perhaps even afterward, who knows? The good news is that for most of us it gets easier. The *really* good news is that you might even get to be a grandparent someday and that can be blissful. You get to play with the children and then they go home. (When I first learned that my daughter was going to have a baby I thought, *I'm too young to be a grandparent.* Now, after a few hours with the little two-year-old dervish, I collapse and think, *I'm too old to be a grandparent.*)

Max was about sixteen months old when his mom and dad dropped him off for a day so they could do some errands. Our apartment has two large walnut doors that open into the living room, and two steps down with a wrought-iron handrail on each side. The little guy, who had been walking for only about four months, became fascinated with opening the doors and trying to navigate the stairs. First, using all his strength, he pulled one of the doors open and looked at the stairs. After a long moment to analyze the situation, he then took three or four small but determined side steps to get to where he could reach one of the handrails, and slowly descended the two steps into the living room. He hardly seemed to notice my highly exuberant cheers and accolades. I was then ready to go on to our next adventure, but Max turned around and decided to master climbing back up the stairs and out of the room. This was not as easy since holding on to a rail, deemed quite necessary, put the door handle beyond his reach while grappling with the challenge of ascending grown-up-size stairs. He stopped, looked a bit concerned, but was clearly undeterred. After a short analysis of the situation he reached for my hand, let go of the railing with his other, and stepped up the stairs to where he could open the door. Again he received, but didn't seem to notice, my enthusiastic expressions of admiration. He closed the door behind him and I now assumed we would be going on to our next escapade, but that was not to be. Max turned back and again mustered up his full strength and opened the doors. He then proceeded to go through the entire journey again—the doors, the rail, the stairs, and the descent. Upon completion, kudos fit for a prince (or at least a grandson). I guess I wasn't completely surprised when he turned, looked at the doors, the railing, and the stairs, and began his return upward, again with the aid of my hand.

Let us now cut to about twenty minutes later and join Max as he completes his eighth up-and-down excursion and prepares for his ninth. By now his little side-step maneuvers are smoother and he has figured out how to venture forth (or should I say "back and forth") without the need for my hand (which I admit I kind of missed). I was now well past my boredom and completely fascinated by his determination and patience. I wondered how long he would continue to work at this. My answer soon came. As he looked at the doors, a barely perceptible smile crossed his face.

He had done his job well. He turned and toddled away, ready for life's next venture.

Later, I thought about how we grown-ups go through life essentially doing the same things Max does. We approach doors, some of which seem to be closed to us, figure out how to open them, pass through, most often with the help of others, and journey forward. When we approach things with a balance of purpose and patience, we tend to move through our days gracefully and with ease. When we lose patience, our vision weakens and we struggle. More often than not our impatience is accompanied by, or perhaps instigated by, anxiety or hurriedness, a sense of not having enough time. So often we feel as if we are trying to get caught up. Caught up with what, we don't necessarily know. Nevertheless, trying to get caught up.

It is the nature of babies to fuss and cry when something doesn't feel comfortable. When we understand that they are doing the only thing they can to communicate with us, we can devote our attention to trying to alleviate the problem, be it hunger, a dirty diaper, or gas pains. It is a responsibility that we can meet with patience and love if we are committed to doing so. No baby is trying to annoy its parents. That is an endeavor not usually undertaken until they reach their fourth or fifth year and not usually mastered until their early teens. Babies cry for a reason and parents usually learn their baby's particular cries fairly quickly and are prepared with the appropriate remedy. Yet there may be times when we simply cannot figure out what's wrong and the crying goes on and on. Then we have to reach deep within for greater perseverance and remind ourselves how much we love this little miracle who has blessed our lives—yes, this very celestial being who is shattering our eardrums and making a shambles of our nervous system. This is undoubtedly more challenging for the single parent who might have to navigate the long night unassisted, finding some way to comfort the little budding dramatic soprano.

Did you ever ask the parent of, let's say, a three-month-old how things are going, and they replied "Really well, he's been sleeping through the night. He's such a good baby." I wonder when it was determined that a baby who sleeps a lot is good, which of course raises the question of whether a baby who doesn't sleep much is bad. It seems an odd way to evaluate the worth of a child. I wonder if research has been done on whether those who slept a lot as babies grew up to become saints, good Samaritans, or philanthropists, while those who had trouble sleeping have tended to become residents in our state penitentiaries.

The question of whether or not one should ever hit a child as part of disciplining comes up often. I am in the "don't hit" camp, but I am probably influenced by my own upbringing which was quite abusive and violent. When one strives for compassion and wisdom, violent actions rarely have a place. However, for those who disagree, I would offer this: if you feel that inflicting physical pain will help correct your child's unskillful behavior, wait at least several hours before carrying out the deed. Nothing will be lost and you will know that you are acting in what you believe to be your child's best interest. The punishment will be about the child's behavior, not your angry reaction to it. By being patient and taking time to wisely consider the alternatives, you might come up with a more creative way to help your child that does not also teach violent behavior. Violence begets violence. Love begets love.

My childhood was spattered with abuse and violence. My mother died when I was sixteen and my father suffered from severe bipolar disorder. He was frequently angry and when not on his medication, which was often, he could be quite violent. With that as my background it is not surprising that as a young adult I caused myself and those closest to me considerable dukkha with my unskillful attempts at meaningful relationships. Yet, with all of that, plus the constantly changing nature of life, I would say that it was my daughter's teenage years that presented my greatest challenge. I was divorced and a single dad, and my ex and I did not agree on much when it came to parenting. That my daughter, Samantha, became the child of divorced parents, and that I was at least 50 percent responsible, was for me a source of regret and considerable sadness.

My ex and I shared custody, and when Samantha was with me we were often battling. We argued about anything that involved the direction of her young life (or the color of my shirt if it happened to displease her). Bright and strong-willed, she was, even then, a presence with which to be reckoned. We argued about what time she was to be home, why she wasn't doing her homework, whether she was experimenting with drugs or alcohol, and why her room looked like a war zone, and those were the casual conversations. One time when she wanted something, I said, "Let me think about it." She demanded, "Why do you have to think about it? You're a parent, you're supposed to know!" Her mom invariably agreed with Sam, so for a few years I was the odd man out, the villain, in this intolerable triangle, which felt as if it were born in Tophet.[4] I doubt that I could have retained any semblance of sanity without the professional counseling I sought and gratefully accepted. More than anything, I was learning about patience.

During this time I met Susanna and eight months later we were married. The playing field evened a bit since Susanna tended to see things as I did. (She's very bright.) Still, the parenting remained precarious and volatile. Then Sam was hit with an illness that landed her in the hospital for two weeks. This must have had a profound effect on her because when she was released she announced that she wanted to live full time with Susanna and me. (My first thought, which I did not verbalize, was: *The last time I wanted to live with a nineteen-year-old, I was twenty.*) The fact that she wanted to live with the *bad guy* and the *wicked stepmother* was remarkable. We have instincts which, if we go with them, can often bring about what could appear to be miraculous happenings. They can even save lives. So Samantha and the newly wedded Susanna and Allan took up residence together for a year. It wasn't always perfect, but it was enormously significant.

Ah, anicca, the law of impermanence; all things are transient, ephemeral, and constantly changing. That which arises will pass away. The parent learns, the child grows. Today, Samantha and I have a relationship more beautiful and loving than either of us could have ever imagined. She and Susanna have also grown to love each other deeply. Samantha is a source of joy and delight in

---

4. Tophet is believed to be a place in the Valley of Hinnom near Jerusalem that was used for the sacrifice of children and other idolatrous worship. After child sacrifice became prohibited the valley was made into a site where carcasses and waste were dumped, and fires were kept burning twenty-four hours a day to dispel disease. Thus, Tophet became a synonym for hell.

my life. We laugh about those difficult years and she says that I probably saved her life. (One of her early boyfriends never made it to his twentieth birthday.) She reverently quotes things I said to her years ago and tells of "invaluable lessons" she learned just by watching her dear old dad.

I am often in awe when I watch Samantha parenting. Her love is unbounded and her patience limitless. She asked me one time if the law of karma means that Max will someday cause her dukkha as she had caused it for me. I said that she will experience dukkha with Max because it is part of natural order. To change our future karma we must change causes and conditions now. Sam's incredible patience with Max bodes well for their future.

When people ask me about how to teach a child patience I tell them to simply be a role model. Live the qualities and virtues you would like to see in your child. It is difficult to explain to a child what patience is. If you practice it they will learn it. Children are imitators. A few weeks ago I saw a woman in the supermarket grab a child by the collar and yell, "I told you we'll go to the park when we finish shopping. Now shut up and be patient or we won't go!" The dichotomy between her words and actions could only be confusing to the child. When you see your child kick and scream out of frustration with a particular situation, think about how he has seen you act in similar circumstances. Make sure you are showing him what you want him to learn. Slow down with children. Let them know the calmer, more patient you.

The Buddha's son, Rahula, was seven years old when he became his father's student. The *Ambalatthika-Rahulovada* Sutra[5] con-

5. Instructions to Rahula at Mango Stone.

tains the Buddha's teachings to Rahula and they are profound. There is an emphasis on the importance of being truthful. "Rahula, if a person feels no shame when telling a deliberate lie, there is no evil he will not do. Therefore, you should commit yourself thus: 'I will not tell a deliberate lie even in jest.'" He patiently taught Rahula to examine his intentions before acting. "Whenever you want to do a certain action, you should reflect on it thus: 'This action I want to do, would it lead to self-harm, to the harm of others, or to both? Would it be an unskillful action, with unfortunate consequences?' If, upon reflection, you know that it would lead to self-harm, to the harm of others, or to both, then you know it would be an unskillful action with unfortunate consequences. Any action of that sort is unfit for you to do. However, if upon reflection you know it would not cause harm to yourself or to others, that it would be a skillful action with pleasant consequences, then that action is fit for you to do."

When we teach a child to be truthful we offer them the gift of an ethical life. When we teach a child to take responsibility for their actions we offer them the gift of an honorable life. When we teach a child patience we offer them the gift of a dignified life.

The lotus fights its way through muck and mud to break through the surface of the water and reveal its remarkable beauty. The greatest wines come from vines that have struggled for decades just to survive. When we plant seeds we need to tend to them lovingly, removing the weeds that can impair their growth, and allowing time for the tender shoots to strengthen. We often can't see any progress and the stems can appear feeble and worthless.

Our work is to provide a favorable environment for the process to unfold. We practice kindness, joy, and equanimity. If we create the causes and conditions that develop goodness, goodness will surely bloom. Be patient; the precious plant needs the warmth of the sun and the day is only now dawning.

> My sister wallows in self-pity. I feel impatient listening to her litany of complaints and tend to tune her out. But when I remind myself that she is suffering, I become more present and listen more intently, allowing her to vent without trying to offer suggestions or solutions. That seems to work better for both of us, though it's difficult for me to accept that I can't fix her problems, or make her less unhappy.
>
> —A communications/public affairs professional

> What makes me impatient is when I have to ask the same questions a million times before I get an answer. [Her remedy: "I pout."]
>
> —A twelve-year-old student

(Author's note: Perhaps I should have interviewed more children.)

The Words We Speak

A Zen master advised: "In times of disagreement, don't side with yourself."

To be mindful is to be aware of thoughts, feelings, and sensations in the body and mind, moment to moment, in an impartial, nonclinging way. The significance of the practice of mindfulness in Buddhist thought can be summed up in these words of the Buddha: "This is a direct path for the purification of beings, for the overcoming of grief and sorrow, for the elimination of pain and distress."[6] To become truly mindful does not come all that easily for most of us. It requires dedication and ongoing practice.

When working with people on communication skills I often suggest a simple practice that requires one to be mindful before they speak. This exercise can be enormously beneficial, especially in conversations that are becoming confrontational. Start sentences with the words *I feel*, and the next word should express how you are feeling at that moment. It requires that we stop, look within, and identify what we are feeling at that moment. The very fact that we have to stop and become aware requires patience and slows what could otherwise become an escalating disagreement with unfortunate results. Sometimes, when I have suggested this exercise, people report back to me that they had already become so impatient that they had trouble identifying what they were feeling at the moment. To help, I have prepared a list of words that can describe how you might be feeling in a given moment. The list is found at the back of this book on page 209. (This exercise invites you to express a feeling, not an opinion. Therefore, to say to another, "I feel you're an idiot" seriously misses the point.)

With practice it becomes easier to identify what we are

6. Digha Nikaya 22.

feeling. We sense when we are losing patience and we direct ourselves to stop and become aware of what we are experiencing in that moment. To do that we must allow the mind to relinquish the position we have been holding so it can focus on pure experience instead. Don't worry about your views not getting aired. We have a much better chance of being heard when we speak calmly and patiently. When our position is based on logic and sound reasoning we can speak gently and quietly. If, however, our argument is based more on personal desire, then we will likely find ourselves raising our voice and becoming aggressive and demanding. Thus, we can see that speaking harshly is a sign of weakness, not strength. If our point is sound and well grounded there is no need for aggression or annoyance. Sometimes we accuse others of not hearing us when in truth they may have heard us perfectly. They simply don't agree. Others are entitled to their views just as we are entitled to ours.

In the Jewish tradition, when a person dies the immediate family members recite a prayer called the Kaddish. It is recited in the presence of a minyan[7] each day for thirty days, or each day for eleven months in the case of a parent, and thereafter at every anniversary of the death. (Details vary within the tradition.) It is interesting to note that the words of the Kaddish are not about death or grief or comforting the mourners; instead the prayer offers praise to God. One view of this might be that Judaism realizes that at the death of a loved one, mourners are suffering

7. A gathering of ten or more Jewish men.

and could lose faith in their God, especially if the deceased was young or died as a result of violence. The words that the mourners are required to speak reiterate faith in their God. The prayer is traditionally spoken in Hebrew. I have several friends who, when a parent died, recited the prayer without knowing what the words meant. Yet somehow the words touched them deeply. We should never underestimate the potential impact of words in any circumstance.

There is probably nothing we could do that would have a more immediate positive effect on our lives and on those around us than becoming more mindful of the words we speak. We are always in relationships and we are constantly communicating. Words have the power to inspire, encourage, comfort, and uplift. Unfortunately, they can also cut, wound, and cause profound, long-lasting sorrow.

There is considerable emphasis in the Buddhist teachings on skillful speech. The Buddha taught: "Skillful speech has five marks. It is speech that is timely, truthful, gentle, purposeful, and spoken with a mind of lovingkindness."[8] Further, the Buddha saw skillful speech as "abstaining from falseness, especially not to lie and not to speak deceitfully; abstaining from slanderous speech and not using words maliciously against others; abstaining from harsh words that offend or hurt others; abstaining from idle chatter that lacks purpose; and abstaining from praising one's self at the expense of others." Surely if our speech reflected these suggestions not only would our words be welcomed as those of a friend but we would likely be spoken to in a kinder and

8. Anguttara Nikaya.

more considerate manner. When someone speaks to us in ways that are in opposition to the above we can find ourselves feeling offended and angered. Therefore, we can safely assume that our speech, if unskillful, will have a similar effect on others.

Distress stemming from our verbal communication could be markedly alleviated, even with those we presently find difficult, if we were more mindful of our words. If you wait for the other person to speak more skillfully you may have a long wait. You can only control you. If the other person responds favorably to your kinder words, that's great. If not, then you get to practice patience. When viewed from an egoless perspective, it is a win-win situation.

We must accept the reality that the causes of impatience travel a two-way street. We need to look at our own thoughts, words, and actions that can lead others to become impatient with us which, of course, can easily lead to our own loss of patience with them. A productive place to start is with becoming more aware of our intention in speaking the words we speak. This is where the practice of mindfulness intersects with the practice of skillful speech. Before we actually speak, we focus on why we want to speak and what we want to say. This helps us get in touch with what is going on within. If we see any negative motivations, we can surround them with mindfulness so that we don't just speak mindlessly. As a result we will become more aware of our words, more thoughtful, more precise. Our words will reflect the person we want to be rather than a reactive individual with a flippant tongue. We save ourselves from saying things we'll later regret. When in doubt as to what to say, remember: it is difficult to put your foot in your mouth when it is closed.

A story often told that illustrates the potential damage caused by words spoken in anger tells of a little boy with a bad temper. His father gave him a bag of nails, took him outside, and told him that every time he lost his temper, he should hammer a nail into the fence. The first day the boy drove thirty-seven nails into the fence, but gradually the number of nails hammered each day dwindled down. He discovered it was easier to hold his temper than to hammer nails into the hardwood fence. When the first day finally came when the boy didn't lose his temper at all, he proudly told his father about it. The father praised the boy and then told him he was now to pull out one nail each day that he was able to hold his temper. The days passed and the young boy was finally able to tell his father that all the nails had been pulled out. The father and son went to the fence. "You have done well, my son, but look at the holes in the fence. The fence will never be the same. When you say things in anger, your words leave scars just like these. When you thrust a knife in a man and draw it out, it won't matter how many times you say 'I'm sorry,' the wound is still there."

Skillful speech entails speaking in ways that are trustworthy, peaceful, comforting, and worth hearing. When you make a practice of these positive forms of skillful speech, your words become a gift to others. People will listen more to what you say, and they will be more likely to respond skillfully (although this is not guaranteed).

Skillful speech has a communicative partner that we call *deep listening*. It's unfortunate that many people with whom we come in contact do not practice skillful speech. However, no matter how unskillful their speech, people are often just trying to communicate feelings that they are uncomfortable expressing. When we listen deeply, taking time to breathe, we can avoid our conditioned reactions that can exacerbate dukkha. Instead, we can respond compassionately to what is beneath the harsh words.

The practice of deep listening can be a highly effective way to develop patience. When we listen with an open mind and an open heart we have a better sense of our interconnected nature with others. Again, it comes back to the simple truth that we all want to be happy. We don't want to suffer. Sometimes the most skillful speech is Noble Silence. For several years I facilitated a weekly sangha in the form I had been taught in the Thich Nhat Hanh community. The rules of the sangha were that during the discussion period no one commented on anything that was said by another. We didn't even say "I agree with you" or "My sister went through the same thing." We offered no suggestions or solutions. All we did was listen to one another. Over time, we saw how often our minds were busy preparing a response when we thought we were actually listening. Knowing that we would not respond dramatically changed the way we listened.

One evening a young woman joined us, and during the discussion period she shared with the group that she had just lost her thirty-seven-year-old husband to cancer. Over the ensuing weeks, she spoke at every session. We often could not understand her words through her heavy sobbing. Sometimes our eyes also filled with tears as we listened, but we did not comment. For me, to witness a person pouring her heart out and going through such suffering while at the same time feeling as if I were offering nothing felt awkward.

Then one day she told us that she had left her various support groups because she was receiving the support she needed from our sangha. We were allowing her to experience and express her anguish knowing there would be no judgments and no fixes offered. We were present for her, listening deeply, bearing witness to her sorrow, holding her in silent compassion. What a lesson that was. Being truly present for another person is the greatest gift we can offer. People don't want us to fix them; sometimes people simply need to be sad. Noble Silence can be truly ennobling, and often it requires great patience. Silence offers us and those around us the spaciousness we need to speak more skillfully. Then, when we do speak, our compassionate, loving self can emerge with a gentle ease.

The most important step in developing skillful speech is to think before speaking (or writing). It is called *mindfulness of speech*. There is little that can improve the nature of our relationships as much as the development of mindful speech.

The *Patimokkha* is the basic code of monastic discipline in the *Theravada*[9] Buddhist tradition. While its vast array of rules is not intended for those outside monastic life, there is much for us lay folk to consider even from a casual read-through. As an example, in the section on speech there are instructions on how to skillfully admonish another. When reading through this recently I couldn't help but think about how quick the mind can be to judge the actions of another. Looking at others judgmentally

9. "*Teaching of the Elders*": the oldest surviving Buddhist school. It draws its scriptural inspiration from the Pali canon, which is generally believed to contain the earliest surviving record of the Buddha's teachings.

paves the way for impatience. Consider the Buddha's instructions to his monastics, here presented in layman's terms:

> One who wants to reprimand another should do so only after considering five conditions in oneself and after establishing five other conditions in oneself: (1) Are my actions pure, flawless, and unblemished? (2) Is my speech pure, flawless, and unblemished? (3) Is my heart of goodwill, free from malice toward all beings? (4) Am I one who has learned much and who bears in mind what he has learned? Do I practice the insight and the letter of the teachings of a spiritual life; do I keep them in mind, practice them in speech, and ponder them in my heart? (5) Have I analyzed those teachings, understood them, and learned them in detail? In addition, these five conditions should also be investigated in oneself: (1) Do I speak at the right time? (2) Do I speak factually? (3) Do I speak gently? (4) Do I speak with words that will be of benefit? (5) Do I speak with a kind heart? Friends, these five conditions are to be investigated in oneself, and the next five are to be established in oneself before one reprimands another.

You and I may not be monastics, but if we were to consider these conditions before judging, criticizing, or reprimanding others, I think we would do so much less frequently and with much greater patience. When we criticize others, the faults we find in them may be a reflection of our own fear. We may fear rejection, unworthiness, or a lack of skill or intelligence. When we look deeply within, with compassion and wisdom, we can connect with our wholeness and our perfection. Yes, we are indeed perfect, even if we need a little work. "Self-love . . . is not so vile a sin as self-neglecting."[10]

Profile in Patience: Lisa

"I really wanted to be a mom," she told me. "Maybe because Bob and I came from families that were warm and loving, our expectations were that our perfect marriage would lead to perfect children." Lisa was like most every other mother-to-be in that she just wanted her children to be healthy.

In a period of three years Lisa became the mother of three children. Her first child, Katie, was born in 1988. "Looking back now, I can see that there was an issue from the beginning. She cried a lot more than other children. She also didn't sleep well and was very colicky. I guess I thought that was just the way it is." At a certain point Lisa and Bob began to realize there were issues beyond the excessive crying. "When she was two she wasn't speaking at all and she was still crying a lot. Her motor skills seemed off as well." Bob's mother, a teacher, was the first to realize something was wrong. Katie wasn't doing the things children her age would ordinarily do. "By the time she was three, I, as a new mother, now with three very small children, was exhausted and trying to figure out what was wrong. People were quick to offer their opinions, saying I was holding Katie too much, or

10. William Shakespeare, *Henry V*, II, iv.

doing this too much, or that too much. But my mother-in-law saw there really was something wrong."

In describing those years, Lisa said there were times when things were okay, but mostly she was exhausted. She recalled, "There was one time I picked Katie up and had an overwhelming desire to shake her, not to hurt her, but just because in that moment I couldn't take the crying. Fortunately, I was able to stop myself. I thought, *Stop, this is your child.* In that instant I realized there are moments in your life when you can be right on the edge."

The family moved to a big farmhouse in Pennsylvania. Bob was working in Manhattan and they assumed he would be able to get a job near their new home. Unfortunately, that didn't happen, so during the week Lisa was alone with her three small children, no friends or family nearby. On the weekends Bob came up, but Monday through Friday it was Lisa alone with the kids. Katie continued to cry a lot and was often out of control. Lisa, in her beautiful farmhouse on a lake, cried every day.

"When she was about three we took Katie to get tested and they said she had attention deficit disorder. That was difficult to hear. We got in the car and Bob cried. This was our child who was going to be a doctor. She was going to be perfect; she was supposed to be perfect. My perfect child was ADD and it was heartbreaking." At the same time Lisa felt unsure about the diagnosis. She thought there was something else wrong with Katie. She began researching; this was before the Internet, so she read every book she could find. She went to support groups for parents with attention-deficit children and would listen to what they said. "I would think, *No, that's not it; that's not what's wrong with my Katie. This doesn't really fit. There's something else here.*"

Katie would scream and yell and destroy things. She didn't sleep well, which meant that Lisa, the mother of three small children, didn't get much sleep either. "Then all day she was so active. It was nonstop activity and getting in trouble and making messes." As Lisa relayed this part of her story, the word *exhausting* came up often. She reached for a tissue box and the bright, cheerful face that had greeted me less than an hour ago now showed signs of fatigue from reliving this journey as she spoke to me.

Lisa felt alone and frightened because she didn't think anyone understood. She recalled, "One time I took Katie to a neurologist. His suggestion was to give her a shovel and send her out in the backyard to dig a hole and use up some of her excess energy. I remember thinking to myself, *The hole she digs is going to be my grave.*" To the casual observer Katie looked normal. They had a diagnosis of attention deficit disorder, but Lisa was certain there was something else wrong. "I was desperate to have somebody confirm my feelings because all I was hearing from people was 'It's your fault, you give in to her too much, you do this wrong, you do that wrong.'" Lisa felt victimized. She was doing the best she could but it was never good enough.

When Katie was five they enrolled her in a regular preschool program, but there were serious differences between her and the other children. She didn't speak well, her motor skills were poor, and she would explode with anger and become irrational, screaming, yelling, and throwing things. Lisa was becoming depressed. "I could not understand why there wasn't an army of people trying to help. I felt so alone; nobody understood." Next she hired a speech pathologist and a teacher to help, but Katie just couldn't fit in anywhere. Then they did get Katie into a special preschool program where she was examined by a child-development team. Their diagnosis: "Developmentally delayed." Lisa thought, *Delayed. I can fix that.* So she hired more people, although she had no idea what *developmentally delayed* really meant. "It didn't matter; at that point we would have done anything. Things just seemed to get worse, louder, and more violent."

At times Lisa felt sorry for herself, wondering why they couldn't be like a normal family. "Why couldn't we go to McDonald's? Why couldn't I go to a store the way others did? When my other kids got older it was embarrassing for them. They would walk away. If we were at the mall and Katie would start I would have to throw her over my shoulder and they would walk away, pretending they didn't know me."

Bob's schedule remained the same, with him arriving at the house in Pennsylvania on Friday evenings and going back to New York late on Sundays. "We would try to have a date night on Saturday, but with three kids, it wasn't easy. Still, we tried to maintain a relationship in the midst of it all. I tried to create some normality for my husband and my other kids, but I felt there was blame on me, burden on me, and guilt on me. During that time I ate my way up to three hundred pounds."

Then, when Katie was ten, Lisa told Bob that she couldn't do it anymore. She needed for them to be together as a family. She and the children had to move back to New Jersey. "That meant giving up my dream house, but there was no other way I could survive. I knew I couldn't do it alone anymore. So we moved back to New Jersey and, again, I cried every day for a year. I felt like a failure."

Back in New Jersey, Lisa took Katie to her original pediatrician, the doctor who had delivered her. "When he filled out a form for the school in which we were enrolling Katie, he wrote 'autistic.' Nobody had ever said autistic before in relation to Katie. In that moment everything changed. Now there was a name, now we could do something. I allowed myself to think I had done an amazing job. There really was something else wrong. As odd as it might sound, I was ecstatic. I was actually happy." Lisa explained, "When Katie was small I had a hard time saying that I had a special-needs child. I didn't think it was bad enough to warrant whatever it was those words meant to me. I couldn't own that, not because it was a sad thing; it *is* a sad thing, but when I think of special needs I think of kids with no legs, in wheelchairs, things much more serious. It was as if I wasn't entitled to say I had a special-needs child. It would be like using a handicapped-parking sticker when I'm not handicapped. I just didn't know. So, in a certain way, I was actually happy when we finally got the diagnosis."

However, notwithstanding the diagnosis, the realities remained. There were three small children to raise and no "fix" on the horizon for Katie. Lisa was again overwhelmed and exhausted. Days became weeks, months became years. When things didn't go the way Katie wanted, she would lose control, often for hours at a time. There would be four, five, even six hours of screaming, crying, and destroying things. "My patience and my approaches morphed over the years. I tried giving her anything she wanted. I tried ignoring her outbursts. It often made me angry. I would wonder why she was doing what she was doing. Sometimes I would yell back. Sometimes I would take things out on others, like snapping at my husband."

I asked Lisa if she ever hit Katie. There was a moment of silence and her eyes saddened. She replied softly, "I did hit her. I probably hit her too hard sometimes. I had those moments when I truly understood how people could cross the line. There were times when I would feel out of control emotionally. I would turn to food or I would yell and scream or throw something. One time I picked up the kids' little plastic table and threw it across the room."

Lisa said that back then she just didn't have the skills to cope. I asked her about now. "I think the turning point for me was learning to surrender to the truth that I could not do it by myself. There was a definite moment of surrender and then an immediate sense of relief. At that time I also began practicing meditation. Not that it suddenly made everything easier, but life was no longer all about one difficulty. I think a big shift happened for me as I began to understand that maybe this was not all about her or all about me. I now understand that she doesn't want to be doing the things she's doing. There's something organic that's uncontrollable. I try not to react, but instead respond from a place of compassion. I remind myself that this is really difficult and it will pass, and then I will get a big hug from her and unconditional love."

I wondered if Lisa was able to maintain that sense of equanimity. "No, not all the time. Katie asks a zillion questions. I like more of a quiet, contemplative life, but if I don't answer a question she'll keep asking it. Even when I do answer, she might ask the same question again and again. Understanding that this is what she needs in order to make her life work, I step back and look at it in a different way. It's just learning to see things in a different way." I asked Lisa if there were times when she was just angry with the whole situation. She said, "Not as much angry as sad. Sometimes I feel sorry for myself. I have my 'pity parties' and I just put my head down and cry, wondering, *Why do I still have to deal with this? Why can't I have an easier life? Why me?*" "Have you come up with answers to those questions?" I asked. "I have some answers," she replied. "I have, why *not* me? Katie is the biggest gift I've ever had and the biggest challenge as well. She's the biggest gift because I've had to learn patience. Honest patience.

"Katie sees the world through the eyes of a five-year-old and there's something magical about that. It's frustrating, but it's also magical. She's a human being and she deserves to have the chance everybody else has, but that's not the way it is. My children have never been to Disney World. We couldn't do those things, but in good moments we could go out in the backyard and play. We don't take that for granted. We don't take anything for granted. We have extremely tender moments, like after a rage, we can have a really tender moment. That's too special to take for granted.

"I now know that patience can be learned. I learned it through compassion. I accept that I cannot be in control. I try to be present to what is, and stay in the moment. That's really all we have. It's a gift and life is short."

CONTEMPLATIONS

Learn this from the flowing waters:
Through mountain slits and gullies,
The smallest streams gush loudly,
But the great rivers flow silently.

— Buddha, Sutra Nipata 720

Treat yourselves and each other with respect, and remind yourselves often of what brought you together. Give the highest priority to the tenderness, gentleness, and kindness that your connection deserves. When frustration, hardships, and fear assail your relationship, as they threaten all relationships at one time or another, remember to focus on what is right between you, not what seems wrong. In this way, you can ride out the storms when clouds hide the face of the sun in your lives, remembering that even if you lose sight of it, the sun is still there.

—Apache tradition

Practice

Honor your relationships by developing listening skills. When conversations are becoming heated, stop and ask the other person if you have heard them correctly, and repeat the words you heard as accurately as you can. This creates a situation in which you must focus on what has actually been said and offers the other an opportunity to evaluate whether they actually said what they intended to say. It also slows down the dialogue, which can allow things to cool a bit.

At the Watercooler

There never has been and never will be a person who receives only praise or only blame. But those who discriminating people continually praise as being wise, compassionate, and thoughtful, those people shine like a coin of pure gold. Even the heavens praise them, even Brahma[1] praises them.

—Buddha, The Dhammapada 228–230

I have had the opportunity to discuss spiritual matters with leaders of many of the world's religious and spiritual traditions: priests, ministers, rabbis, imams, dharma teachers, and others. While they speak from a wide range of perspectives there is one point upon which they all seem to agree: spiritual practice is not easy. We don't necessarily feel the challenge while we sit in church, temple, or on the meditation cushion. There we are usually surrounded by like-minded people with tradition and a sacred atmosphere soothing our being. It is when we step out into the world and tread the highways and byways of our

1. In the Hindu tradition, Brahma is the creator. In Buddhism, the Hindu deities are respected and sometimes mentioned anecdotally in the teachings, but they are not worshipped.

daily lives, crossing paths with every manner of sentient, and not-so-sentient, being, that our spiritual self is subjected to the glaring light of the "real world." For many, nowhere is that real world more challenging to our patient self than the workplace.

The manner in which we support ourselves was seen by the Buddha as so significant that he made *samma-ajiva* or "right livelihood," one of the steps of the Noble Eightfold Path. This core teaching in the Buddhist tradition is seen as the path out of an existence of dukkha and leading to the experience of awakening. There is a preponderance of research that confirms what most of us already know: we spend the majority of our waking hours involved in some way with our livelihood. We get up in the morning, choose our outfit for the workday, travel to work, do our work, return home, and often bring our work home with us, be it physically, mentally, emotionally, or all three. For some, a drink after work temporarily releases the tension of the workday or provides an opportunity to vent about what can't be verbalized in the office.

Unfortunately, the same studies that track our daily involvement with our work also reveal that many people are not happy with their work situation. When we look deeply we can see the source of that unhappiness. On some level, many of us expect our work to be the fount of our happiness. However, if we expect our job, or for that matter anything outside of ourselves, to provide our happiness, we will be disappointed. Instead, we need to find joy within and then bring that joyful feeling to our work. That is not to say that the way we earn our livelihood cannot be fulfilling and pleasurable. It can be, and hopefully is, but only we ourselves can provide inner peace and sustainable happiness.

It is in the workplace, perhaps more than anywhere else, that the entire Eightfold Path converges. At some point *skillful view*, *skillful intention*, *skillful speech*, *skillful action*, *skillful livelihood*, *skillful effort*, *skillful concentration*, and *skillful mindfulness* are all needed so that the way we earn our livelihood might feel gratifying and joyful. It is on the job that we have an excellent opportunity to walk our spiritual talk. The workplace can also provide an opportune setting for the development of patience.

Most of us need an appropriate way to support ourselves and those who depend on us. The Buddhist teachings on skillfully earning our livelihood suggest that our work not cause us to act in opposition to five basic precepts: to do no harm; to take nothing that is not freely given; to not engage in sexual misconduct; to not lie or speak harshly; and to not abuse intoxicants. Those in a position of authority must be particularly mindful when commenting on the work of others. Harsh or rude words can do serious harm to another human being. They also demean oneself and demoralize the workplace. Unskillful speech destroys motivation and does not produce better results. People want to feel appreciated. Correcting errors with patience and encouragement has consistently been shown to be the most effective approach. To kill the spirit of another through abusive words or deeds is unskillful action, and it also happens to be bad for business.

Taking small items such as paper clips, rubber bands, or pencils for personal use is taking what is not really yours. Justifying such actions with thoughts of being underpaid in a multibillion-dollar corporation does not change the underlying nature of the act.

To use one's authority or position to take sexual advantage of an employee is not only in opposition to basic moral conduct, it is also illegal. When other employees sense that kind of activity has taken place or that advancement has been awarded because of sexual favors there is likely to be anger, fear, and disruption even if allegations cannot be proven. Even a hint of innuendo should be avoided. The use of intoxicants on the job, or anyplace else for that matter, clouds the mind and diminishes the possibility of clear thinking. Businesses don't function well under such conditions.

Acting in unskillful, unkind ways in the workplace and expecting to enjoy a peaceful and happy life away from the job is foolish. We cannot compartmentalize our lives. We can live in denial, believing we are getting away with small indiscretions and unskillful actions, but the inner stress will take its toll. People wonder why they are so impatient with their loved ones and don't see the connection between the suffering they cause themselves at work and the angry flare-ups that erupt from them at home. We can convince ourselves that the delusions we fabricate at work are necessary so that our children can have a good education, but we fail to consider what our actions are teaching our children now.

Our livelihood should not be in conflict with our moral principles nor interfere with our spiritual well-being. Any job can be skillful livelihood as long as it does no harm to the person performing it nor to any other being, but if our work causes us to experience greed, anger, or deception, we will feel stressed and we will suffer. Even if this stress is subtle, an edgy impatience may be our constant companion. Of course the same circumstances that could cause one of us stress and anxiety could be experienced by another as an opportunity to practice patience and compassion. To know who and where we are, we need to be mindful, awake, and reflective.

We can elevate any honest work to honorable livelihood and, unfortunately, the other side of the coin is that even the noblest profession can be dishonored by greed, laziness, impatience, or delusion. Medicine, law, religion, academia, and the arts have all been disgraced often enough that we cannot assume they are automatically glorified professions. They are made honorable, or not so, by those who practice them.

On June 2, 2010, Armando Galarraga of the Detroit Tigers baseball team pitched what appeared to be a perfect game, one of the rarest feats in all of sports. However, on what should have been the last out of the game, he was charged with giving up a hit when the umpire erroneously called the Cleveland Indians batter safe at first base. Videotapes clearly showed what most people felt they had already seen—the batter was out. Upon seeing the tapes after the game, the umpire tearfully acknowledged his mistake: "I just cost that kid a perfect game. I thought he [the batter] beat the throw. I was convinced he beat the throw, until I saw the replay." The umpire made a mistake and baseball rules do not allow for the ruling to be overturned. The record books will show there was no perfect game. Mistakes happen, this one unfortunate for both the pitcher and the umpire. However, by the next day, what was drawing the most attention was not the blunder, but the extraordinary grace and patience with which the pitcher was handling the situation. He never questioned the call, never argued, and after the game had only supportive words for the umpire who, in turn, did something umpires and officials rarely do: he admitted his mistake. More important, he had done his job with impeccable integrity; he called the play as he saw it. He was never tempted by the possibility of being part of a historic moment. The next day he was out there again doing his job, booed by the fans (that's apparently their job), but respected by all.

Having to do business in the work environment of another where you have little or no control can often be stressful and frustrating. For instance, trying to convince a utility company that you have been overcharged can surely test one's patience, as can being informed that the warranty covering your rapidly warming refrigerator expired yesterday. Waiting in a doctor's office when they are behind schedule can be particularly trying since you may have arrived for the appointment already feeling anxious. Calmly, and perhaps firmly, expressing that you would like to be treated with respect is often appropriate and effective. Patience is not passivity, indifference, or a lack of self-caring. True patience is grounded in wisdom and compassion, and compassion is not complete if it does not include oneself.

If our intention is to do as little work as possible for as much money as possible, we can harm ourselves and others, and we can demean our work. But if our purpose is to perform a useful role in society, support ourselves, and help others, then our work can enhance our happiness, and we will feel successful. When we use our minds, our hearts, and our hands to create and be of benefit to others, we can transcend greed and ego; we can act with wisdom, embodying exemplary ethical values. Often this takes but a moment of patience. Other times it requires the "patience of a saint."

One time when I was on retreat with the Vietnamese Zen monk Thich Nhat Hanh, who was already in his seventies, a woman asked, "Thây,[2] you lead retreats all over the world, you write books, you teach in universities, you consult with world leaders, you address congresses, parliaments, and corporations, you are a busy spiritual leader—what do you do for fun?" Thây thought for a moment and replied, "Everything I do is fun."

For several years we had a house in Connecticut where I had a workshop in the basement. One day a tool distributor told me that he had bought a stock of old kitchen knives from a company in France that was going out of business and asked if I wanted some. It seemed like an opportunity to acquire some useful antique items at a good price so I bought an assortment of eight. Our kitchen knife block was already full and a search of the local stores and the Internet did not reveal any blocks large enough to hold our new collection. So I decided to build a large knife block. After all, how difficult could it be?

It turned out that it could be quite difficult for one of my modest skill. For one thing, I had never thought about how they got those slots into the block. I wandered through the kitchen departments of several large stores surreptitiously investigating the structure of their various knife blocks. I eventually figured out that those slots weren't actually cut into the blocks after all, but were grooves cut into pieces of wood which were then carefully laminated together. Just to make things more challenging, the better knife blocks were made of rock maple which, as the name suggests, is not that easy to cut. Undaunted by my lack of training (in other words, I had little idea what I was doing), I began the project. A mere three months later I had a rather handsome large

2. Vietnamese for "teacher."

knife block that now holds all our kitchen knives. Every time I look at that block I enjoy it, not with an ego-filled mind, but an admiration for something well made. Being constructed of solid maple it should be around for many years to come, although how far can we be from the day when all kitchen slicing and chopping will be done by one simple handheld laser?

There was in our lives at the time I made that block a man who wasn't particularly skillful with his speech. Seeing the knife block he said, "That's nothing a Boy Scout couldn't make." It wasn't a gracious comment but it didn't change the work I had done and it didn't take away from my satisfaction. With patience, I had met a challenge and done a good job. In the workplace and in all aspects of life, not everyone will appreciate our efforts, so it is important that we work in a way that we ourselves can feel good about our own endeavors. We want to find our satisfaction in the work itself. Then we release our efforts into the world without any sense of grasping or possessiveness. Your actions are your only true belongings. As the Austro-German poet Rainer Maria Rilke so beautifully points out, there is no material thing that we can truly call our own:

They will say "mine" as one will sometimes call
the prince his friend in speech with villagers,
this prince being very great—and far away.
They call strange walls "mine," knowing not at all
who is the master of the house indeed.
They still say "mine," and claim possession, though
each thing, as they approach, withdraws and closes;
a silly charlatan perhaps thus poses

as owner of the lightning and the sun.
And so they say: my life, my wife, my child,
my dog, well knowing all that they have styled
their own: life, wife, child, dog, remain
shapes foreign and unknown,
that blindly groping they must stumble on.

This truth, be sure, only the great discern,
who long for eyes. The others will not learn
that in the beggary of their wandering
they cannot claim a bond with any thing,
but, driven from possessions they have prized,
not by their own belongings recognized,
they can own wives no more than they own flowers,
whose life is alien and apart from ours.[3]

The virtues of free enterprise can become distorted by greed and delusion. With an unstable economy some may feel obligated to stay at jobs that send them home heartsick, physically sick, and weary of spirit. No wonder we easily lose our patience. There can be an unbearable gap between our spiritual being and our secular existence, yet we feel we need the security of that particular job. To be mindful entails examining the path we are traveling and making choices that alleviate suffering and bring happiness to ourselves and those around us. Even in situations that are not ideal there is potential for satisfaction. The workplace is where we can use and expand our intellect, talents, and

3. From *Poems from the Book of Hours* (Babette Deutsch, trans., 1941; 2009).

skills; it is where we can accomplish something that no one else on earth can do quite the same way.

Put out full effort,
but remember that not everything that matters is matter.

The workplace is different in an important aspect from other areas of our lives. In our personal relationships we work out and slowly establish our role with others. Usually we do this subtly, simply, and comfortably. In marriage we negotiate specifics as to who will be responsible for what and who will be in charge of what. Sometimes the details are discussed and sometimes they simply evolve. These social relationships are essentially equal. At work that is rarely the case. Someone is in charge and the others follow instructions. If those instructions are offered graciously with an invitation to make suggestions, that can create a pleasant atmosphere, but the relationship is still not equal. It can't be equal because that is not its nature or intent. Unfortunately, that can lead to feelings of powerlessness, a sense of having no control. That sense of impotence can be a breeding ground for discontent and impatience. That's where the practice of meditation can be invaluable. Over time we learn that we have complete control over what matters most—our mind, and therefore our perceptions and how we experience things. The experience of pleasant, unpleasant, or neutral is the consequence of perception. We add opinions, evaluations, and judgments, and therefore the quality of all experience is controlled by us. That is truly powerful; that is control.

My wife enjoys coffee (tea for me, please), and for years I watched her prepare a cup of instant coffee each morning. I occasionally asked if she wouldn't prefer her coffee freshly brewed and she would say that it's pretty much the same and not worth the extra fuss. Then we stayed in our friends' house in Santa Fe while they were away for a couple of weeks. They had a simple coffeemaker and I asked Susanna if I could make her a cup of fresh coffee. When she drank it she admitted it was far superior to instant, but she didn't know if she wanted an additional chore each morning in her already busy schedule. I told her I would love to make fresh coffee for her each morning and although she didn't want me to add something to my schedule she finally agreed. I began to call it "my job." I love doing it: carefully measuring the water, the coffee, and the milk. It's so completely ordinary, but I love doing it.

There is a story of an elderly watchmaker, his face withered, but his vision keen. He worked all day with tiny parts like jewels, springs, gears, and screws, and he approached each of them with reverence. He focused mindfully on each little part and handled them with dignified simplicity. In each moment nothing was more important than the part he was handling. He joined each to the next meticulously, always taking enough time for every aspect of his work, always mindful of the tiniest detail, always patient. After each part was perfectly secured he allowed himself a moment to appreciate the subtlety of his work. Then he moved on to the next part, again mindfully handling each tiny object. Because of his calm, single-pointed focus there was a feeling of peace and serenity in his workshop. It was as if a special event was happening as he worked with each watch. Every evening he left his shop with a deep sense of peace and satisfaction.

This type of relationship to one's livelihood is rare today. We seem to honor the mediocrity produced by multitasking even as science questions its veracity. We're too busy to give our full attention to anything. Our constant rushing tills the ground for tension and impatience. By contrast, a person taking her time is rarely, if ever, impatient. We suffer in many ways including missing any joy that our work could yield. We bring that feverish mentality home and wonder how it could be that she who was our precious little infant yesterday is sitting there today filling out college applications. We can instead patiently create the spaciousness that allows us to be present, fully present with our work and our colleagues. In this way we honor our spiritual self and the precious moments of this life.

> When I can be mindful enough, I take a deep breath and try to ground myself by being in the present moment. I also try reminding myself that I may not be good at the task at hand and that I need to be gentle with myself.
>
> —A PSYCHOLOGIST, AUTHOR, AND MUSICIAN IN FLORIDA

Technology

Let us take a speculative look at next week's tech page in our local newspaper: *The capacity of today's basic desktop computer, now a gazillion, trillion, lotsabytes, is already overloaded. However, it is rumored that hard drives will soon be replaced with invisible microthreads that can hold the equivalent of 26,860,464,832 encyclopedias per millimeter. Beta tests show that this capacity should satisfy the average user for about three months although the speed, approximately 200 trillion calculations per nanosecond, is already considered sluggish by the geek community. This is actually seen as good news for the technology industry, which thrives because we are so easily convinced that we need the newest, fastest, slickest model, which has been shown to be as much as fourteen-tenths of a second faster than the archaic model we bought three weeks ago.*

We live in the "Information Age," with more facts, figures, data, knowledge, advice, direction, guidance, dirt, and dope available to us than the brightest among us could possibly absorb in several lifetimes, and it keeps coming. My young friends cannot imagine how life was managed before the advent of the cell phone and they even have me believing that I must regularly call someone, anyone, to say, "Hi, I'm walking down the street." When I told one of them that I can remember life before television she asked if my father ever let me keep a brontosaurus in our backyard.

We have experienced greater technological advancements in the past thirty years than in the entire history of humanity. The potential benefits are staggering and almost beyond comprehension. The sharing of the latest medical advancements with up-to-the-minute methodologies for treating previously "incurable" illnesses and conditions, as well as effective practices for saving the planet are just the tip of the iceberg. Technology is here and it is only going to become more and more integrated into our lives. The sum total of human knowledge is about to be at our fingertips.

Yet, as has been pointed out by masters from the past, knowledge can be an obstacle on the path to wisdom. It is so easy to become convinced that we *know*. What will be the cost technology extracts from our innocence, our *beginner's mind*, our need to think calmly? As we become more tied to our technologically miraculous devices, when will we develop our compassionate self, which is best done in direct communion with other beings, not through Facebook or Twitter-type relationships? In August 2010, the *New York Times* carried a story about how robots are becoming more and more involved in treating hospitalized patients. Doctors raved about the potential, but no one commented about how we are losing the irreplaceable healing power of the human touch.

The more we meld with the rapidity of the digital world the less time our minds have to actually assimilate information. We are already rushing about at a pace unimagined by previous generations. How do we harness the remarkable technology of our time so that it serves the common good and not the greed, hatred, and delusion that haunt humanity? How can this lifestyle be reconciled with an intent to live mindfully, with inner peace and the dignity and grace of patience?

Patience requires a slowing down, a spaciousness, a sense of ease that may be getting swallowed up by bits and bytes. Did you ever notice that the patient person never appears to be rushing? Patience has all the time it needs. Rushing never has enough. A turbocharged workplace breeds impatience, and with it discontent, disharmony, distress, discomfort, and disease. We must find ways to let technology work at its pace while we work at a pace that allows us to breathe comfortably, and with the least possible stress. Then we can have workplaces that are physically, mentally, and emotionally healthy. This type of atmosphere invariably proves to be most productive.

Technology offers us a unique opportunity, though rarely welcome, to practice patience. Computers, printers, fax machines, tablets, copiers, and cell phones, remarkable though they may be, will have hiccups. They crash, they break down, they can no longer be charged, kind of like human beings. Only, since we pay for the electronic devices (unlike the bodies we one day found ourselves inhabiting), we expect them to work. We wonder in awe how the electronic marvels know the exact, most inconvenient moment to go comatose. Too often we take them for granted, as we do our own bodies. Because of our deep reliance on technology in so many areas of our lives, breakdowns can really test our patience.

I had accepted an offer to write an article for a prestigious magazine. The deadline was close, but the piece was flowing well. I was about three-quarters finished when suddenly my ultrareliable Mac computer balked. I have been a Mac user from the beginning, in the mid-eighties, and have become fairly Mac-savvy, but could not spot the problem. Finally I did a restart. I knew my article might be lost but my auto-backup system, which I had set to back up every hour, would have a copy. When the computer rebooted the problem still existed. I finally called my computer guru, Peter, who asked the pertinent questions, praised my taking all the appropriate steps, and then said, "I don't think it's the computer. Is your backup device showing on the screen?" (This is why we have computer-genius friends.) "No," I said, "it's not." Peter replied, "Your backup device died. It happens so often. They're the weak link. I can get a new one over to you within an hour." "That's great," I said. "Will we be able to recover my work from the dead backup?" "No, I'm afraid not," said Peter. "When those devices crash they lose everything."

Years ago, in a moment such as that, it would not have been a pleasant experience to be around me. Today, in times of adversity, I find myself so grateful for my years of meditation practice. I closed my eyes and quietly looked at what was going on in my mind and body. There was annoyance and disappointment but it passed rather quickly. I then felt at ease with no sense of having to rush. I decided that this mishap gave me an opportunity to write a newer and better version of the article. I practiced walking meditation for about twenty minutes and, true to his word, Peter arrived with the new backup. I have no idea whether the new version of the article was better than the old but the magazine folks were pleased, as was I. This was an important lesson for me. At this point in my life my work is about sharing the dharma through teaching and writing. The article I was writing was, interestingly enough, about patience. I have worked on patience within myself for many years. To experience the benefits of that work while writing about it was exhilarating and joyful, like watching a cycle complete itself. The tech misadventure, while annoying and disruptive, was simply causes and conditions coming together to create a new opportunity. There was no ego, no "self" that had done something wrong to cause the breakdown. There was just the experience. Then mindfulness, patience, and back to work.

I recently installed in my computer an app that is designed to "gently remind you to take a break on a regular basis." I figured it could be of value since I don't tend to take breaks often enough. I also assumed there would be a difference between my taking breaks when I chose to do so and when some device demanded it, and I was curious to see how I would respond. The app would surely intrude at times when I didn't want to be interrupted. Sure enough, I found it to be an obtrusive bother the first few hours, its only saving grace being to afford me an opportunity to practice patience. However, I've actually developed an appreciation for the little intrusions and I now find them quite welcome (most of the time). In truth, it is hardly necessary to purposefully create opportunities to practice patience. There's rarely a shortage.

In 2007, several friends and I founded the Community Meditation Center. As we formed our first board of directors, I told each prospective member that I intended our board meetings to be held in a calm, retreat-like atmosphere. They all had previous board experience and may have doubted whether there could be such a thing as a peaceful board meeting that would at the same time be productive. Yet productive we have been. To date we have exceeded our projections for each year. Attendance has grown steadily, to the point where the CMC has become recognized as a vital spiritual presence on Manhattan's Upper West Side. We don't charge a fee for classes. We exist entirely on the traditional practice of *dana* (generosity), which means that those who attend support the CMC as their means permit. The generosity of our board further supports the organization so that we can maintain that policy.

To date, our board meetings have been held in a calm, creative atmosphere as we originally intended. We address issues before they become problematic. We don't expect our voting to always be unanimous, although it often is, and so far we have never had a contentious moment in a meeting. I believe there are several reasons for this. We begin meetings with a silent meditation for about twenty minutes. This allows space for each of us to become present, get in touch with what is going on within, and bring the mind to a more focused state. We then set an intention for the meeting, which is usually a simple statement reminding ourselves that we are there to serve the CMC and its members. We do a short check-in during which we each share what we wish of what is going on in our lives. Within the meeting proper we have a policy that when someone is speaking they will not be interrupted. Therefore, I think we have a sense that we are being heard when we speak. I believe we are each truly interested in what the others have to say. Mostly, we are interested in being of benefit to those who rely on us, the CMC members. There is always laughter and occasionally tears as we are comfortable enough with each other to speak our deepest truths. We have created a workplace built on respect, truthfulness, kindness, and compassion. I have watched it happen; it can be done.

In Buddhism, giving alms is a way to show respect and to support monks and nuns. The Buddha and his disciples would teach and, in return, receive alms in the form of food and medicine. Today this practice continues as people offer dana to their dharma teachers, those who offer the teachings of the Buddha. One time a certain gentleman invited the Buddha to his house to receive alms. When the Honored One arrived at the gentleman's house, instead of offering alms, he ranted and raved, offering abuse and obscene language. The Buddha calmly listened and then asked his host, "Do you often have visitors in your house, sir?" "Yes, indeed," he replied. "In what way do you entertain them?" asked the Buddha. "I offer them a magnificent meal." "May I ask, sir, what you do if your guests refuse the food?" "Why, then it remains mine." "Well then, good sir, you have invited me for alms and instead offered me abuse, which I decline to accept. Therefore, it still belongs to you."[4]

In this story the Buddha shows no interest in retaliation or reprisal. His attitude is simply and calmly nonacceptance of what was given to him. He hears the words, but with such spaciousness it is as if they evaporate and have no impact. He is like a solid rock not shaken by praise or blame. It takes a person of well-practiced patience and compassion to be able to hear harsh criticism and insults being directed at them and still maintain equanimity. It is not pleasant to be the recipient of unkind comments, justified or not, and it is certainly not enjoyable to have harsh language directed at oneself. For many, a word, a tone of voice, or a scornful glance can trigger memories of childhood abuse. Yet with effort and patience those wounds can be healed. Then they no longer color our views and trigger conditioned responses. Those "buttons" become disengaged. We can actually feel genuine compassion for our attacker. We see that one who is abusive, unkind, or unfair is suffering greatly. This is the heart of patience. This is patience with a heart.

It used to be that we could say, "I'm unhappy at my job so I'm leaving." For some, that may still be an option. However, for many the repercussions of the global economic crisis that

4. Akkosa Sutra; Samyutta Nikaya 7:2.

greeted the twenty-first century will be felt for years to come. There simply are fewer options. We can no longer blithely say if work conditions aren't pleasant, we'll leave and get another job. We may be in a situation for some time where many of us have to stay at jobs in which conditions are not ideally suited to our temperament. The reality of feeding and sheltering ourselves and our families remains with us in these difficult economic times. Therefore, learning the art, the skill, the virtue of patience in the workplace may be of greater importance than ever before. Even for those in ideal work situations there will always be bumps and difficult people with which to deal. On the job, we relate to people, to technology, to life, and to ourselves, all of which will, at times, present challenges. Peace lies within. No one can take that from you.

> When there is a technology failure I usually have to focus and solve the problem quickly, which requires letting go of all blaming and thoughts of impending doom. I find comfort in the fact that it has happened before, and the problems, though inconvenient, were overcome, and no one died in the process.
>
> —An audio engineer

Profile in Patience: Noël Carmichael

I met the tall, soft-spoken Noël Carmichael a few years ago when she came to me to study meditation. She was twenty-five years old and had just survived a rare form of ovarian cancer. I had been working with her for about a year when one day she told me about a job offer she had received. It involved going to Tanzania to build a factory that would produce Plumpynut, a high-nutrition food that could save the lives of thousands of malnourished children. She knew I had been to Tanzania several times and asked what I thought of the idea. I chose not to talk about the wave of anxiety and concern that had swept over me, but rather expressed my interest in how she felt about such a move. She said she felt honored to be asked, although she didn't really understand why someone who had never been to Africa and certainly knew nothing about building factories would be selected. Yet I wasn't at all surprised to learn a few weeks later that she had accepted the offer.

Knowing that she had a satisfying career in the arts and had just come through a difficult and frightening illness I was curious about why she accepted the offer. She explained "During my months of recovery from surgery, I discovered inside myself an intense desire to help the less fortunate of the world. It was as if my gift of life needed to be used to improve the lives of others. I wanted to travel and do good works." In one of our many ensuing e-mail exchanges she wrote, "I can't say I ever actually made a deliberate decision to change careers or even move to Africa. I was just seeking an opportunity and one appeared. It seemed like a natural flow of cause and event. I actually had to get online to make sure I knew where Tanzania was. I knew nothing about the country, not even its location."

More recently she told me, "I first went to Africa full of open-minded ignorance and wild dreams about being one person able to positively affect the lives of others. Were it not for this naïveté and passion, I probably would never have gone. Thinking now of what I had to go through for two and a half years, it is hard to believe what we've accomplished. I went to Tanzania to build a factory that could produce a specialized, fortified food that when given to children on the brink of dying from malnutrition could save their lives and restore their health. From the time I became involved in this project, I approached my work with a great deal of urgency. Every day wasted meant more lives lost."

When I had been to Tanzania it was always as a visitor photographing wildlife. I could not imagine what it would be like to conduct business in such a poor, laid-back environment. Noël confirmed my concerns. "I sometimes think that my whole existence in Tanzania has been one big lesson in patience. In the United States 'wasting time' is viewed as sinful and success is often measured by how much one can accomplish in a day or in a year. Not only am I from that culture but when I lived in it I fully embraced that notion. Now I live in a country where 22 percent of all children are suffering from acute malnutrition, thousands of them at a life-threatening stage. I expected my cause would be met with the same urgency that I felt. This has, for the most part, not been the case."

She described, as constant obstacles, bureaucratic nightmares, corruption, and an apathy that stems from general acceptance of early death for children and adults. "One of my challenges," she said, "has been to understand this way of thinking without adopting it myself. What from the outside looks like apathy and hopelessness, from the inside looks like acceptance of reality. It is difficult to balance my passion for bringing positive changes with patience, and the fact that the changes will not happen as quickly as I want."

Noël had continued with her meditation in Tanzania and we consulted by e-mail fairly regularly, working on specific points of her practice. I asked her about how she practiced patience when dealing with bureaucracy, corruption, and apathy. "One way has been by relinquishing or letting go of the way I think things should be done. I guess giving in is the source of a lot of my patience these days." I was glad she said "giving in" rather than "giving up." Giving in can be seen as part of the negotiation process in business when each party yields a point so that progress can be made and the endeavor moves forward. It is the art and practice of relinquishing. As Noël explained, "It comes from my ability to accept the way things are done here, even if I totally disagree, am disgusted, offended, or otherwise critical of it. I can still be all of those things but on some level I have to accept in order to be a part of it. In order to do the work I came here to do, I need to be a part of it." The frustrations she dealt with were endless:

> It's very difficult to get accurate information here, even when asking the same questions of two people working in the same organization. The procedures I was given for how to register a business were different every time I asked. I was led in circles, often being asked for bribes along the way by people hinting that they had a way to get things done faster or to make things 'official' without all the hassle. When official processes are as convoluted and drawn out as they are here, I often feel that the system is set up that way intentionally to create an environment where those of us trying to do the right thing will give in to the bribery.

She was often brought to tears by the frustration of not being able to accomplish the most basic tasks to get the project going.

> I was so angry that people blocked my work in order to profit from it, especially since we were here trying to do something to help *their* country. It was so disheartening. It was only having a sense that I was doing something truly needed that kept me motivated. I try to avoid aggressive confrontations, an attitude which served me well during these encounters where I thought people deserved a piece of my mind or a good smack. You just have to go along with it, this is how things are done here.
>
> Some of these situations caused me to feel very judgmental. Things are so inefficient and unnecessary. I didn't understand why we had to go through all this. But I tried not to judge. I'd think, *If I stop judging I can understand the purpose.* This has been somewhat successful and I have grown some in my appreciation for the formal structure of this society. But I still think it is ridiculous how they make unnecessary paperwork and formalities so important. The difference is that now it bothers me less. I expect to wait in line. I expect poor customer service. I expect to accomplish half of what I set out to do each day. Somewhere deep inside, I am still frustrated, I've lost the battle. Or perhaps by letting go of wanting things my way I've actually won. I don't know, but it is the best way to get things done.

Noël fell in love and recently got married in Tanzania. I wasn't surprised to learn that she and her fiancé climbed to the top of Mount Kilimanjaro to tie the knot. After all, you can experience so much more when you are 19,340 feet above the earth.

CONTEMPLATIONS

It is natural for immature people to hurt others.
Being annoyed with them is like
resenting a fire for burning.

—SHANTIDEVA, BODHICHARYAVATARA

There is an old saying, not just made up today:
"People will blame you if you say too much; they
will blame you if you say too little; they will blame
you if you are absolutely silent." No one
engaged in the world escapes blame.

—BUDDHA, THE DHAMMAPADA 227

Practice

Regularly, throughout the day, stop for a few minutes, close your eyes, and do a detailed body scan starting at the top of the head, proceeding down to the toes. Then bring your awareness to the sensations of the breath and just observe for at least five breaths. Remind yourself that your mental and emotional health are important. During these breaks do not answer the phone or respond to e-mails or texts. When possible, take a short walk outside. This practice is for your mental health. Do not allow yourself to believe you are too busy.

If you work at a computer, install Time Out Free (or an equivalent). It is free, as the name suggests, and will invite you regularly to stop what you are doing for an interval of your choosing. Try setting it to activate for a period of ten seconds every fifteen minutes. In a tangible way, this little app forces you to practice patience. No matter what you are doing, it interrupts and you can practice learning to appreciate the interruption rather than simply being annoyed, not to mention that the minibreaks are great for clearing the mind.

What Would a Sage Do?

Anger brings with it great misery,
anger churns up and disrupts our thinking;
it is not understood by most
this frightening peril that lies deep within.

—Buddha, Itivuttaka 3.88

When I first encountered the Bodhicharyavatara,[1] the great work of Achariya[2] Shantideva, the eighth-century Indian Buddhist philosopher, it left me feeling overwhelmed and under-accomplished. Yet at the same time I was deeply moved by its extraordinary wisdom and compassion, and the depth of insights into anger and patience. Through the years I have become more familiar with the text, but still harbor no delusion of fully grasping all the subtleties or the profound depth of its

1. "The Way of the Bodhisattva." A *bodhisattva* is an enlightened being motivated by great compassion and a wish to attain Buddhahood for the sake of benefiting all beings.

2. Achariya: teacher, guide.

understanding. Shantideva offers teachings on patience that are as insightful and relevant today as they must have been when he wrote them thirteen centuries ago. My appreciation for the Bodhicharyavatara has been enhanced enormously by the various times I have heard His Holiness the Dalai Lama offer teachings on the text. His Holiness has said the Bodhicharyavatara has been the highest inspiration for his ideals and practices. I am motivated here by a belief that every opportunity one has to experience these teachings can only be beneficial. May I humbly suggest paddling slowly; the waters here are deep.

What is possibly the best-known section of the Bodhicharyavatara, sometimes called the Prayer of Shantideva, has for years been part of my everyday life:

For all those ailing in the world,
Until their every sickness has been healed,
May I myself become for them
The doctor, nurse, the medicine itself.

Raining down a flood of food and drink,
May I dispel the ills of thirst and famine,
And in the ages marked by scarcity and want,
May I myself appear as drink and sustenance.

For sentient beings, poor and destitute,
May I become a treasure ever-plentiful,
And lie before them closely in their reach,
A varied source of all that they might need.

My body, thus, and all my good deeds besides,
And all my merits gained and to be gained,
I give them all away, withholding nothing
To bring about the benefit of beings.

Like the earth and the pervading elements,
Enduring like the sky itself endures,
For boundless multitudes of living beings,
May I be their ground and sustenance.

Thus for everything that lives,
As far as the limits of the sky,
May I provide their livelihood and nourishment
Until they pass beyond the bonds of suffering.

The numerous accounts of Shantideva's life may well have been embellished through the centuries, but the teachings remain profound and revelatory. He was the son of a king. When his father died it was assumed Shantideva would reign, but the night before he was to be enthroned, Manjushri, the Bodhisattva of Wisdom, came to him in a dream. *My son,* he said, *this throne is my seat, and I am your teacher. How can we two sit on the same throne?* Shantideva interpreted the dream as meaning that it would not be appropriate for him to become king. He left his home, relinquishing everything that was his (a parallel to the Buddha himself) and went to study at the great university of Nalanda, where he became a monk.

He diligently studied and meditated, but he did his work on

his own, in private. Therefore, Shantideva's great insights were unknown to the other students, who saw him as lazy and useless. They called him *Bhusuka*, which means "he who eats, sleeps, and shits." The students felt he was a disgrace to their exalted university. They plotted against him and asked Shantideva to offer a teaching, assuming he didn't know anything worth sharing and would leave the university humiliated. Several times Shantideva refused to teach, but when his teacher insisted he finally agreed.

To ensure that Shantideva would be embarrassed, the other students built a high throne without stairs, from which Shantideva was to teach. Surely he would look foolish and awkward trying to ascend the throne. But when it was time for him to speak Shantideva simply appeared on the throne. No one saw how he got up there leaving some to believe he had levitated. He then recited his Bodhicharyavatara from memory. When he was approaching the end, it is said that he again levitated and rose up until he was completely out of sight, yet his voice was clearly heard to the end of the teaching. (As mentioned, some embellishment may have become part of the account, but it is still a great story.)

Some commentators suggest that Shantideva may well have had the students at Nalanda in mind when he wrote the Bodhicharyavatara, wanting to teach them about the true path of wisdom and compassion. Others say he wrote it as a guide for himself. Today we can view it as having been written for all of us no matter our religious or spiritual beliefs, if any. It can certainly be seen as a secular discourse. For our purposes, it is a great gift that a major portion of the teaching is devoted to the development of patience and the extinction of anger.

A Flash of Anger

Shantideva begins discussing patience with the dramatic statement: *A single flash of anger can destroy all the good deeds, the generosity, the kindness we have practiced over thousands of eons.* Whether or not we believe that we have lived previous lives is not essential to appreciating the profound nature of this statement. Surely we have all seen and felt in this lifetime the destructive power of "a single flash of anger." Loving relationships can be damaged to the point where it may take months or years to rebuild them. Apologies can help, but we can never take back the words we have spoken. No matter how we justify our anger, how right we believe we are, the result is likely to be the same. Acting while angry invariably causes dukkha, no matter how warranted we believe our anger to be. Shantideva invites us to open our eyes to this reality, that we might alleviate our suffering and that of those around us. The message is direct and simple: don't speak or act while in the throes of anger.

Perseverence

He points out rather fervently that *there is no wrongdoing like hatred* (some translations even say that there is no *evil* like hatred), and also that *there is no strength of character, no discipline, like patience.* Therefore, the suggestion is to commit oneself in every possible way to developing patience. Anger fills the mind with anguish and stress, feelings that are then experienced in the body as well. When we are angry we can't enjoy those things that ordinarily bring pleasure. We become consumed and can't get a peaceful night's sleep. Even those who love us, who depend on us, back away. ("Leave Daddy alone right now; we'll speak with him later.") We find ourselves alone, surrounded only by the flames of our wrathful thoughts. Therefore, as intelligent beings, when we realize that anger is our enemy we don't feed it. When it arises we acknowledge it; we watch it carefully, but we don't let it gain a strong foothold. We don't look for ways to justify its presence.

Distress

Shantideva addresses the cause of anger and refers to it as the *fuel of mental misery*. Specifically, it is *not getting what we want and having to endure what we don't want*. Here, it seems to me, he is echoing the Buddha's words describing the causes of dukkha: "Association with what is abhorred is dukkha; separation from what is loved is dukkha."[3] Shantideva says we should *completely destroy this fuel [the causes of anger] because it has no other purpose but to cause us harm, suffering, and grief.* We can so easily become attached to our desire to have things our way even when it is clear that it is not going to happen. This clinging and grasping fan the initial embers of anger caused by frustration or annoyance. An essential part of the development of patience is learning to sense this type of discontent at its embryonic stage so that we can cool the flames before they gain strength. However, even raging fires can be put out with the skillful use of patience as a cooling agent.

3. Dhammacakkappavattana Sutra; Samyutta Nikaya 56.11.

JOY

Shantideva's joyful nature emerges and he declares that *no matter what may befall me, I will not disturb my jovial state of mind.* Further, *when unhappy I never accomplish what I want and the worth of my good deeds becomes diminished.* Here Shantideva is reminding us that we can at any time examine our mind and make the decision to stop our negative thinking. We don't have to be carried away with our "add-ons" and our scenarios. We don't have to create mental stress. We all have dispositions and personalities and we seem to have innate tendencies either toward seeing more of the bright side or more of the dark side. We want to be mindful of habit energy that pulls us toward negative thinking and focusing on the unpleasant side of things. As the Buddha said, "What we are is a result of our thoughts. What we are arises with our thoughts. With our thoughts we make the world."[4] Life presents many challenges, we don't have to distend them. As is often said: in life pain is inevitable, suffering is optional.

BE HAPPY

The pragmatic Shantideva then points out that *if there is something that can be done about a troublesome situation then why be unhappy? If there is nothing that can be done about the situation, then what's the use of being unhappy?* (One time when my daughter was a little girl she said to me, "Oh, Daddy, you're so darn logical." I wonder why that comes to mind.) The logic here is so

4. Dhammapada 1.

straightforward and obvious and yet we cannot always get to that logical place as quickly as we would like. With practice, however, we train the mind to be with what is happening as it is happening in the moment. That is part of the development of patience and it can free us from a great deal of dukkha. Patience is often misunderstood to be some sort of static, emotionless state. That is far from the truth. Patience allows us to be fully present with what is going on within and around us so that when action is advisable we can make wise decisions. When action would be fruitless we can likewise see that clearly and work toward relinquishing our annoyance and frustration.

Learning

There is nothing that doesn't become easier with familiarity. Therefore, by learning to deal with small pains and inconveniences I learn to be patient with greater ones. Shantideva is suggesting that we can use life's minor inconveniences as a training ground for developing patience. As an example, practicing patience when the person sitting next to us in a restaurant is speaking loudly into their cell phone may be easier than when a colleague at work suddenly launches verbal abuse at us for no apparent reason. *I already know how to bear with minor distress such as insect bites, hunger, and thirst.* Everyone has some level of patience, including those who claim to have none. We can enhance and develop our smallest experience of patience by being mindful and appreciative of ourselves when we have been patient in what might otherwise be passed over as an insignificant moment.

Clarity

Even when wise people suffer, their mind remains clear and equanimous. Suffering, unlike physical pain, is created in the mind. We are very much what we think. Therefore, we want to change any conditioned thinking and reactive patterns that can deprive us of the freedom of a calm and peaceful mind. Thoughts arise naturally; it is the function of the mind. As we learn to be mindful of the thought process itself, we see how thoughts are constantly arising and dying away. We can remain calm as we notice how pleasant thoughts can lead to desire and craving, and unpleasant thoughts can bring aversion, fear, and stress. We do not have to cling to our thoughts, we can simply be aware of them.

The Value of Suffering

With a slight shift in perspective Shantideva points out that *suffering can have value since it can undermine arrogance, develop compassion, and reveal the negative consequences of unskillful actions, thus making skillfulness more appealing*. We can live life anesthetized by complacency. The suffering brought on by a major illness, the death of a loved one, or the complete loss of financial security can provide the kind of thunderbolt that causes us to look at ourselves and the world as we have never done before. Being brought to our knees by such events can be the stimulus for introspection and spiritual growth. Battling a life-threatening illness or experiencing a major loss can open us to the suffering of other beings. We see that we are all connected and truly need one another. The worthlessness of our self-centered actions becomes unappealing and we appreciate more fully the value of our good deeds.

IMPATIENCE

Just as I don't become angry with inanimate things even though they might cause me pain, why should I be angry with living beings? Their actions also only come about through causes and conditions. Now Shantideva really begins to challenge us. He points out that we don't get angry at insentient things that cause us suffering. (I will take a small exception to that: more than once I have cast a dirty look toward a table in my living room when I have banged my shin into it, suggesting that it was the table's fault for being in my path. It seems easier than admitting that I was careless again.) He goes on by noting that we can quickly lose our temper at a fellow being who we feel is causing us suffering. Yes, all phenomena come about due to causes and conditions, but we could argue that sentient beings can make choices and should know better. However, that bypasses the essential point that the person who harmed us is, like us, subject to extremely complex factors, including conditioning and emotions. Shantideva wants us to stop and look within rather than react with our conditioned behavior. This does not mean becoming a doormat, but rather responding with wisdom and compassion even in heated moments.

Sometimes we say, "Well, of course I lost my patience when that happened. Who wouldn't?" This thinking suggests that a particular action could have a specific reaction inherently within it. When we look deeply we see that this is not the case. One time I was teaching a meditation class and near the end of a sitting, someone's cell phone rang with a sound just like the bell I use to end each meditation. I kept my eyes closed even as I heard movement begin in the room, suggesting that people thought the sitting was over. Then, as they saw that I was still in meditation the room quieted down and everyone continued their practice. I could almost feel the annoyance, and the judgmental minds thinking how mindless of someone to not turn off their phone. Nevertheless, I found the "false alarm" rather amusing and I was told later that there was a broad smile on my face. When I rang the real bell to end the sitting there was considerable laughter. Even when everyone around us is annoyed and impatient, we can remain happy and peaceful.

SERENITY AND INNER PEACE

When we experience an enemy[5] *or a friend acting in a way that is improper, we remain serene and remind ourselves that all things arise from causes and conditions.* Shantideva reminds us that we can never know the complete story about anything. Rather than react with harsh judgment, stay cool (modern translation). We would want others to do the same for us. Such equanimity may require great patience; we call it "the way of the wise."

Since none of us wants to suffer, if things happened according to our wishes then no living being would ever suffer. We all want to be happy. That being so, why do we do the same things again

5. The term *enemy* refers to someone with whom we are not getting along at the moment.

and again that we have seen lead directly to dukkha? As an example, once we learn that being in conflict with others leads to loneliness and stress, wouldn't we want to seek peaceful solutions rather than clinging to a need to be "right"? On a global level, when will we see that war has never led to enduring peace? "Hatred does not cease by hatred. Only by love does hatred cease. This is the eternal rule."[6]

The Foolishness of Anger

If it is the nature of unskillful beings to cause harm to others, being angry with them would be pointless. It would be like resenting fire for burning. If however, it is the nature of sentient beings to be good and wholesome, it would still be pointless to be angry at them for their momentary faults. It would be like resenting the sky for the falling rain. Shantideva presents us with two choices: either people are essentially bad or they are good. If they are bad, then accept the fact that their actions will be offensive and injurious. Don't expect an oak tree to produce maple leaves. Just as it is wise not to get too close to a raging fire, it can be wise to practice judiciousness in the form of right association and avoid those who seem bent on disruption. If, on the other hand, people are good, then their offenses are temporary. They come about due to conditions that are constantly changing. Even the beautiful blue sky sometimes drenches us with an unwelcome downpour. Pause, be patient, and the sun will again shine, in both the unbounded sky and the hearts of those around us.

6. Buddha, The Dhammapada 1.5.

GRACIOUSNESS

Shantideva suggests a little humility be practiced when he says, *Surely, in the past I caused similar harm to others as is now being caused to me. It is only fair that I receive some of the same.* I am not at all certain that many of us would so graciously acknowledge the fairness of harm being caused us simply because we might have committed a similar offense in the past. Yet let's not miss the important point: we can develop patience even for those who harm or offend us. We do that by learning to see the bigger picture. There is always more going on than we can see in any given moment. We may very well have been as unskillful at some time in the past as the offender is now. Perhaps it was in a previous life—how can we know? The full nature of karma is complex, but even a perfunctory understanding of basic cause and effect principles offers insight into Shantideva's point. This is not about punishment, or getting even, or "tit for tat." It is common sense. Every action is a cause that will lead to an effect. If karma and rebirth are not within your beliefs, then practice mindfulness, compassion, and lovingkindness anyway because they will bring happiness to you and to those around you. Consider with compassion the complexity of the human condition. We can look at and be amused by our foolishness. We can also learn how to create a more enduring happiness.

FINDING FAULT

Communication travels a two-way street. *Both the weapon used by the offender and my body that receives the offense must come together to cause my suffering. He brought the weapon and I the body. With whom should I be angry?* Is Shantideva daring to suggest that we play a role in our own suffering? Isn't it always the other person's fault? I think he is being kind in implying that we are only partially responsible. This is a tricky point. It is how we perceive the events, people, and conditions around us that determines our life experience. Another person may strike us and cause us physical pain, but only we can cause our own suffering. This is an important distinction. We are responsible for our own happiness and peace of mind. We need to be patient with the world around us and the world within us.

Illogical

It is our childish actions that cause us dukkha. Even though we don't want to suffer we are so attracted to the causes of suffering. Why then are we angry with others? Shantideva is a lot kinder than Dr. House, television's favorite abusive genius, who would probably call us all "idiots." We believe we must do more, be more, have more. Our home should be bigger, our car should be faster, and our bodies should be thinner/fuller/curvier/flatter or whatever is on the cover of the latest fashion magazine. We don't want to suffer yet we seem intent on perpetuating the conditions that bring about what we don't want. We are attracted to the very thoughts, ideas, and actions that cause us dukkha. We rush as fast as we can today, convincing ourselves that if we do we will then be able to slow down tomorrow. We become workaholics so that we can send the kids to the best schools, only we never get to see the kids, except perhaps for a few minutes when we are exhausted.

THE MIND

If my mind develops the grace of patience, I shall be spared grief in the future. I am therefore saving myself, but what about my foes? If I retaliate their harm with harm, it will not benefit them or me, and all my good works will be negated and the virtue of my patience would be lost. As we develop patience the mind becomes our greatest ally. We can make calm, wise decisions; we can enjoy inner peace, but those around us may still be caught in the snare of impatience and an angry mind. They may attack us when their suffering boils over. We ourselves are not yet fully enlightened beings so we might want to retaliate, but when we stop for a moment and consider how the other is suffering we can be compassionate. Compassion is not pity nor does it come from a position of superiority. It is kind, forgiving, and wise. When we retaliate with attacking words or actions, we undermine our efforts to develop greater compassion and lovingkindness. We are always stimulating behavior patterns and strengthening habit energy. We want to minimize our slipups and allow ourselves to feel the joy of our more skillful actions.

INTENTION

Since abusive words cause no injury to my body, why then, O mind, do you become so angry when I'm subjected to unkind comments? When I was teaching singing I would remind my students that no matter what the critics wrote in the newspapers, the performance they gave was what it was. No words, no opinions, no praise or criticism could change it. They had to know for themselves whether it was a performance about which they could feel good. All of us are in the same situation. The karmic imprint of an action is determined by the intention that drives the action, not the result. Know your intention. Be willing to accept honest criticism. At the same time, to be compassionate to oneself might require disengaging from a source of abuse. That is called "right association."

Words

Others may dislike me, but that scorn cannot harm me[7] *in this or future lives, so why does it distress me so? Do I think it will prevent my attaining greater wealth? I know I must leave everything behind except for the consequences of my actions.* Shantideva acknowledges the pain of rejection, but also points out that the words of others cannot change the reality of what is. When we speak of causes and conditions we include our upbringing and the wiring of our particular "buttons." The right words (or perhaps the wrong ones) can easily push those buttons and lead to distress. Often it takes great effort balanced with patience to disengage them, but it can be done. To refer back to our TV friend Dr. House, he calls his colleagues "idiot" so often that over time the word loses its meaning. If anything, they see that it is House who is acting like an idiot and they no longer take his comments personally. Even if the unkind words of others could prevent our attaining greater wealth, we're not taking it with us anyway, so don't let unkind words bother you too much.

---

7. The actual translation is more colorful, something like "cannot chew and swallow me up."

Caution

When a house is on fire and the flames are spreading to another house, the wise are swift to remove the flammables that would cause the fire to grow. Similarly, when anger and hatred are arising we should quickly remove from the mind those thoughts that are stoking the fire so that our good deeds not be damaged by the flames. Our anger is fueled by the stories we create around actual events and situations. It is difficult to be with just a bare phenomenon itself, since the pull of our emotional experience is so strong. A simple example might be to see that a flower has petals and a stem. That is bare experience. "Beautiful" yellow petals and a "graceful" green stem incorporates our add-ons. This example is innocuous, but how quickly and easily we can create storylines around someone's glance, or dress, or haircut. We are usually unaware that we are doing it, yet how adamantly we can cling to our scenarios. Shantideva warns that it is this clinging to views that can cause the fire of anger to grow out of control. He advises that we remove that fuel, especially the rigid belief that we are right and others should see things our way.

Singing Praises

Shantideva asks, *If someone finds pleasure in praising the excellent qualities of another, why then, O mind of mine, do you too not praise and enjoy the pleasure of doing so?* Years ago, in my days as a professional singer, when the first of my friends made his debut at the Metropolitan Opera, I remember being excited for him and cheering loudly when he took his curtain call. At the same time I experienced a certain feeling of envy which an understanding friend described to me as my wanting my cookies too. Earlier, when looking at the Brahma Viharas, we considered the quality called *mudita*, which means altruistic or sympathetic joy. I actually like to translate it as "harmonious joy." (Not as accurate perhaps, but I like the overtones of *harmony*.) Mudita is about experiencing joy and delight in the good fortune and well-being of others. The practice of mudita not only loosens the reins of resentment and endless desire, but also opens up many opportunities for happiness since we rejoice not just in our own good fortune, but in that of all beings as well. We open up millions more opportunities for happiness. It is not easy because sometimes someone else's good fortune might appear to be at our expense. However, the practice is all-inclusive and we learn how to see beyond our own desires, release our envy, and truly rejoice with others, even those we don't particularly like. (I said it isn't easy.)

Comparisons

I have made mistakes and acted unskillfully, often feeling no remorse. Why then do I compare myself with those whose actions are so much more skillful? This is not an invitation to a guilt trip. We have all performed many acts of kindness and compassion and likewise have, at times, slipped up. While it can be helpful to associate with and emulate the actions of spiritually advanced beings, comparing ourselves to others is not likely to be beneficial. The implied suggestion is that we be mindful of our actions and notice that some deeds create dukkha and some bring happiness. It is too easy to become inflated if we view ourselves as superior to others, or deflated if we believe ourselves to be inferior. It is better to focus instead on our endeavors.

Thoughts

Even if misfortune were to come upon your enemy, would it be a reason to be happy? Your most fervent wish for their unhappiness will not cause them harm. Suppose, however, that the suffering of your enemy actually did come about due to your wishes, is that reason to celebrate? If you were to say, "Well, now I feel satisfied," could there be a more dreadful way of achieving satisfaction? What we want to consider here is how our thoughts influence our mood and our actions. In every moment that the mind is focused on petty or vengeful thoughts, we are not at peace. Conversely, when our mind is inclined toward thoughts that are kind, compassionate, and generous of spirit, we experience a sense of joy and serenity. Unless you have some type of psychic power your mean-spirited thoughts will not harm others, but they can be quite unhealthy for you. Remember, the mind is everything. As you are thinking, you are becoming.

Curious Blessings

I could view those who speak disparagingly of me as protecting me from the torment of impatience and anger. They are blessing me by affording me the opportunity to practice patience. Several years ago I read a book by a contemporary philosopher that I found so annoying I had to read it again to find out why it irked me so. I realized that I connected on a deep level with what the author was saying, but that I was not ready to make the intense commitment he was suggesting. The above section of the Bodhicharyavatara likewise seems so logical and "right on." Nonetheless I know that I am not yet all that grateful when someone speaks poorly of me behind my back. I can be patient, even compassionate, because I know that my "enemy" is experiencing dukkha, but gratitude is often quite a few steps behind. This doesn't feel to me like a failing as much as an awareness that I still have a way to go. If I feel discouraged I look back at how far I have come. If I feel a bit inflated I look at how far I still have to go. It is about balance and, at times, it can feel like standing on a seesaw, both challenging and fun.

Agitators

I should welcome all enemies, for without them I cannot advance on my path to awakening. Only because these partners presented themselves was I able to practice patience. Again, Shantideva presents us with logic that we might at first want to reject. Welcome those who provoke us? Really, now. Yet no one can practice patience in a vacuum. In addition, the more patient we become, fewer there will be who annoy us. Therefore, we can silently thank those provocateurs who present themselves as our practice partners. One of my students told me she finds herself "blessed" often with the opportunity to practice patience by those who speak loudly on their cell phones in elevators or restaurants. "I'm doing better," she said. "I am aware of my annoyance much more quickly and I no longer feel a need to comment, even when a devastatingly wicked remark comes to mind." Surely gratitude is not far behind. The person well skilled in patience also knows how to act with compassion and wisdom when it is advisable to put a stop to abuse and wrongdoing.

To help us with this challenging concept, that of honoring those who provoke and annoy us, we remind ourselves that we are practicing patience, we are not encouraging the offenders to continue their rude and abusive ways. This is an important distinction. When we react to provocation with anger we are escalating the unpleasantness. When we practice patience we are moving toward peace, for both ourselves and the other. Do we actually want to verbally thank the offender? Perhaps not. A simple, silent thought of lovingkindness might suffice and in many cases would be wiser. The thought could be a sincere *May you be happy.* This is your practice, intended to benefit you. Remember, when an abusive person becomes happier it is good for you.

The decision is always up to us as to how we will respond to the other person's anger. If we have previously responded with our own anger we know what that feels like. Now if we can practice patience instead, as Shantideva suggests, we might surprise ourselves by developing a depth of compassion and wisdom we had not previously known. That level of experience can be joyful and deeply satisfying. It is certainly different from the turmoil stirred up by our own anger.

Royal Rewards

Even if there were a king who, becoming angry, could cause me terrible agony, could this pain be equal to that which I would cause myself by making other beings suffer? And even if I were to please such a king he could not bestow enlightenment upon me. That reward comes naturally to those who bring joy and delight to others. The harshest sentence a king could impose would not cause us the suffering of our own impatient, angry mind. It often appears that the actions of others are the source of our unhappiness but, in truth, it is our relation to, our perception of, those actions that determines our experience. Likewise, the most luxurious gifts a king might bestow could not bring the inner peace and happiness that only we can awaken within ourselves through our friendly, kind, and compassionate relationship with others. For most of us it takes time to fully realize the truth that our greatest happiness already exists within. How can we not allow our hearts and minds to open to the needs of others? We are all in this together. Our happiness is inextricably tied to that of all beings.

Patience

In this lifetime patience brings beauty, good health, and honor. With patience well developed I shall enjoy peace and a long life. Shantideva's final effort addresses our ego and foretells of today's scientific findings. No one looks or feels attractive when angry. A grumpy, tempestuous person will have very few friends. The inner churning caused by impatience and anger is the breeding ground for stress and illness. There is no illness that is not exacerbated by stress. One who is patient glows with an inner radiance. Be mindful of not striking back at small offenses because such retaliation serves to reinforce our aggressive tendencies, which then grow and become more potent. Patience with minor matters helps develop patience even in life's most challenging moments.

We have journeyed a long way with Shantideva. We see that the people, events, and conditions outside of ourselves are not the cause of our happiness or unhappiness. It is our perceptions, our experience of these phenomena that create our quality of life. We can easily give undue weight to the words of others if they massage the ego, or, conversely, if they confirm any feelings of unworthiness. Admiration can feel good, but don't become attached to it. It is like a sand castle on the beach, lovely perhaps, impermanent for sure. The vicissitudes of life can take us on a stomach-churning ride. How easily praise can become blame, fame can become obscurity, pleasure can become pain, and gain can become loss. Praise and esteem can feel good, which is fine, but don't look to them for inner peace and lasting happiness. They don't enhance the merit of our deeds nor do they increase our well-being. Our actions speak for us, and they speak loudly.

We should remain focused on our journey, acknowledging our advancements with humility and proceeding enthusiastically where there is still progress to be made. With patience we allow the world around us to be as it is, and experience all things with ease, graciousness, and forgiveness.

Profile in Patience: Venerable Metteyya

The PBS special *The Buddha* brought the delightful Nepalese Buddhist monk Venerable Metteyya into the homes of many thousands of viewers. I remember watching the show and being charmed by his graciousness and enthusiasm. So when I was invited a few months later to meet him while he was visiting New York I felt honored and was pleased to accept. I was even more pleased when he accepted my invitation to teach at the Community Meditation Center. We spent quite a bit of time together during that week and I had the opportunity to discuss with him the monastic view of patience and his own experience dealing with impatience and anger.

One of the first thoughts Metteyya offered was that the Buddha saw the virtue of patience as being so important that he included it in the list of ten *Paramis*, or "Perfection Practices."[8] These practices are intended to help one achieve the goal of enlightenment. Then, with a flash of his amazing smile, he said, "But I know that you know that because I read your book about the Paramis."[9] He continued, "The Buddha's approach is not just to develop patience in order to deal with particular situations that may come upon us. It is a quality that when cultivated will

8. The Paramis: Pali (Sanskrit: *Paramitas*), generosity, morality, relinquishing, wisdom, effort, patience, truthfulness, determination, lovingkindness, and equanimity.

9. *Pocket Peace* (Tarcher/Penguin, 2010).

create a framework, like a backbone, upon which qualities such as compassion and effort can develop."

When Metteyya began studying he didn't think patience was all that important. Now, as a scholar, he views the quality of patience as one of the most essential aspects on the path of awakening. He sees the Buddha's view of patience as a mental quality that helps address any situation with proper awareness, without reacting based on our conditioning. We observe a situation as it is, clearly, taking a moment to stop, analyze, and then make the best possible choices. He said:

> Buddha taught that patience is one of the most important qualities for developing all other skillful qualities. As an example, you cannot employ effort if you don't know how to balance the energy of effort with the calm of patience. It is like controlling a wild horse with the reins. In that simile, the reins are patience. Otherwise, Buddha says you will burn out your energy. He taught that patience is an essential step before you can reach wisdom. When I try to understand beyond the traditional teaching, I see patience as a kind of spaciousness, an essential spaciousness, where we analyze a situation and its associated feelings and our action is then infused with proper thinking. So Buddha really said that patience is one of the basic qualities that should be in every step we take.

Now Metteyya travels a great deal and has to contend with the same airport delays, canceled flights, traffic jams, and other inconveniences as the rest of us. I was curious about how he handled life in the secular world.

> From the outside it appears that the monastic life is different from the layperson's life, but the inner element, the inner chemistry is almost the same. The monastic life was designed by Buddha in a way that always tests the quality of patience. In fact, not just tests it, but really provokes it. For example, in traditional Buddhist communities we rely on people's generosity. Some monks, even Buddha's disciples Ananda and Sariputra, went to Buddha and proposed that if they had a fixed place where they could get a meal it would allow more time for them to work. The Buddha rejected the notion. The whole idea was that by going to people's homes for alms it created more conditions with which to contend. Even today, when we go for alms we're not allowed to ask, "Please give me food." We just stand in front of people's homes holding our bowls. We don't ask for anything. Often that tests our patience. Sometimes people are busy and they don't see us. Buddha said these are essential parts of the practice of patience. If people ask if we'd like tea, as Buddhist monastics we are not supposed to say yes or no. We simply accept what is offered. If they ask would you like this tea or that tea, we're not supposed to say anything. We simply accept what is offered.

I recalled how only an hour earlier I had offered Metteyya a cup of tea and several flavor choices. He had merely looked down without responding. We now both laughed and he assured me it was no problem. I promised to spend more time familiarizing myself with the details of the monastic code. I also admitted to a moment of impatience with myself because I have studied the code and I knew better. Metteyya's graciousness made quick work of any embarrassment I felt.

Metteyya is deeply involved in social service work. At the age of fifteen, with his dharma mother, Bodhi Shakyadita, he founded Metta Children's School in Nepal which provides free education for over eight hundred impoverished local children. When he started working what tested his patience was what he saw as a paradox in the teaching.

> Buddha says that human life is the most precious gift, that we should rejoice in it. He also says human life is very short, like a flick of time. When I put these two together I saw that my most precious life is very short. I was doing social projects like running schools and I found myself always driven by a deep feeling that I had very little time. So I felt I had to try to do the best I could in any situation. That made me what you call a workaholic. So I would want to do good work, but in our country when I would try to move people along and want a particular job done within a certain time, it never worked out well. We have a notion that we call "Nepali time." It means that if you invite someone to a meeting at nine o'clock and they appear at nine forty-five, then they are on time. I had a hard time with it. I lost my patience quite a few times. I was angry with my team of volunteers, trying to tell them we had to live on English time.

I asked, "You grew up with Nepali time. Weren't you used to that?" Metteyya said,

> I did grow up with it, but somehow I was never part of it. In my mind if I was impatient with the slowness I thought I was doing things right. If I was angry I had good reason to be angry

because life is precious and time was running out. Then I learned there could be another way. What made me review my actions was that I started perceiving that when something went wrong and I reacted to it negatively, I would lose two or three more hours, sometimes even days. That obviously wasn't productive. I thought, *No matter whose fault it is, it's me who's losing the time, it's me who's losing this precious human life. It is not wise to act so emotionally.* I could tell my people that this or that was not good but still do it with patience. Whatever has been done wrong is already done, I cannot do anything to change it. If my mind is calm, balanced, and I haven't lost my patience, at least I am able to deal with it. So that has become my approach. Whenever something goes wrong, I say whatever has happened is past. What is next is important. If I lament on what has already happened and lose my patience I'm losing my next moment. This approach has helped me a lot.

Just before coming here I was stuck in the Frankfurt airport in Germany, in the plane, not moving, for about four hours. It was snowing really heavily. Sometimes when you are stuck in a seat all you can do is meditate. So I started and I saw impatience coming. Then I looked out a window at what was going on and I saw people cleaning up the runway. But by the time they finished, the wings were frozen, so they would bring the deicer and spray them. When they were done with that, the runway needed to be cleaned again. They did that back and forth three times. I thought, *Why don't they think more skillfully? Have two teams working together. One on the runway and one on the wings.* I was able to see the ignorance that was causing the situation but

> I wasn't angry with it. I was able to see what would have worked better and then I relaxed. There was nothing I could do to help.

What I was hearing from Metteyya was that monastic life does not change basic human emotions. No matter what one's training and practice, impatience can still arise. It's how we deal with it, how we relate to feelings that arise, that is significant. He confirmed.

> Yes. Also Buddha said that patience is like the gatekeeper that keeps the door locked between the world outside and the world within. By world within he means the *sankharas.*[10] Sankhara means "patterns," "habitual patterns," "conditioning," what we call the *subconscious conditioning*. Sometimes they take over and we react based on that conditioning, even without knowing it. So Buddha says patience is the gatekeeper between these two worlds and if we lose patience, we give full access to those habitual patterns to dictate or influence our actions. That can be a dangerous situation. Also, indulging the sankharas makes them stronger whereas when we don't indulge them they lose their power.

Metteyya felt that the issue of impatience doesn't get much priority in people's daily lives, which he saw as a serious error. By contrast, he pointed out that people address physical illness and discomfort rather quickly, giving it complete attention: even simple colds, coughs, and slight fevers.

---

10. *Sankhara* can refer to anything formed or that comes about through conditions, or thought-formations within the mind.

"Not that they shouldn't," he said, "but I've rarely heard people addressing whether there is anything wrong with their level of impatience and anger. They don't address the internal and external damage being done. In Buddhism, what we say is that there is one medicine that treats all kinds of pain and suffering. It is mindfulness. So what we need is to develop mindfulness of our own selves and especially about our inner workings. We want to become aware of the relationship between our impatience and how we create negative situations. Buddha says that becoming aware of the energy of impatience is like touching the tip of the problem. Mindfulness itself works like a catalyst. Somehow it starts to change impatience.

"Also, from the Buddhist perspective, everything can be personified, even abstract ideas are given a personality. Impatience is known as a demon with many arms and hands and this demon can easily grow more arms and hands. Symbolically, what it means is that once we lose our patience we are training our mind to do it again and the mind believes it is okay to do it again and again. I think this is a very powerful image to see how the mind works. When we see that image we realize there is an urgent need to deal with our impatience. We see how our life is influenced by it."

Metteyya's final words had a sense of urgency.

I think we need to become serious about the quality of patience and the harm of impatience. If we have a tendency to lose our patience, it can do more harm than an illness. It damages our relationship with our family and friends, children can be especially harmed, and the hurt can live on for a long time. Buddhist advice is that we sift through our inner environment, our thoughts and feelings, and identify this disease of the mind. Impatience can be like fever in epidemic proportions. When it arises there is heat. When we manage it, it becomes cool, like soothing water. You start by simply thinking about how impatience affects your life. You look deeply. Yes, I think that should be the starting point.

Bodhi Shakyadita

Venerable Metteyya is supported and encouraged by his Dharma Mother, Bodhi Shakyadita.[10] In this role she provides for his material and medical needs so he can be free to concentrate on his spiritual path. In return, she receives guidance and teachings from her *Dhammaputta*, or "Dharma Son." Bodhi's life is complex, not only because of looking after Metteyya, but also because she is a Buddhist nun, and holds a full-time position as an environmental scientist with the federal government of Canada. I was curious about whether these roles might be conflicting at times in ways that tried her patience.

Yes. More often than not it's the little things that catch me off guard. As an example, in Canada I live with my mother. When I come home after a long day at work the first thing I need

10. The Dharma Mother concept originated in the time of the Buddha, but today is practiced only in Nepal, Burma, and Sri Lanka, where she is called *Dayaka Amma* or *Datu Amma*.

> to do is take off my shoes and coat and use the facilities—you know, basic things. My mother, on the other hand, has been home alone all day and wants to talk and visit. I can lose my patience. I think I have an underlying expectation that she should understand that when I come home I need ten minutes for myself. It's not her needs but my expectation that causes the problem.

I wasn't all that surprised to learn that a nun's response to that kind of situation wouldn't be that much different from that of a layperson. She added,

> Sometimes I react with a snappy answer and am a bit short. I'm not as calm, peaceful, and polite in my response as I would like to be. Then when I realize that I'm not being very compassionate, I might take a step back and either focus on my breath or the sensations of my body. I see that I'm feeling agitated. So as soon as I realize what's happening I just take a moment and retreat.

Knowing how bad I can feel if I lose my patience and don't handle a situation well, I wondered if, as a monastic and a meditator with many years of experience, Bodhi experienced similar feelings. "Definitely, but over the years I have come to accept that just because I'm a monastic, and just because I'm a Buddhist doesn't make me perfect. I'm not enlightened. I'm working on the path and I'm committed to it deeply. I'm much more accepting now but I still have a long way to go."

I believe the same is true for the layperson who wants to practice a specific tradition or simply wants to develop a deeper sense of inner peace and joy. We need to have a certain ease within ourselves, accepting that, from time to time, we will slip up. We are living life in human form this time around, meaning that we are at once perfect and imperfect, powerful and vulnerable, nothing, and in that nothingness, everything. Bodhi added,

> Yes, absolutely. We can be upset for hours or we can accept our humanness, come to peace with it, and then be a wiser person, more compassionate and kind. It's better than losing time in judgment and self-bashing. We really have to develop the mindfulness to spot our impatience. If we can't detect it, we can't do anything about it. So mindfulness practice, meditation practice, can lead us to be aware of the various emotions that can cause us problems, impatience certainly being one of them.

CONTEMPLATIONS

Where could there possibly be enough leather
With which I could cover the entire earth?
However, covering the soles of my feet with leather
Would be equivalent to covering the entire earth.

Similarly, it is not possible for me
To alter the course of external events,
But if I supervise this mind of mine
There would be no need to control anything else.

—Shantideva, Bodhicharyavatara

Knowing well that the other person is angry,
one who remains mindful and calm,
acts not only to heal himself,
but the other as well.

—Buddha, Samyutta Nikaya 11:1.4

How poor are they that have not patience!
What wound did ever heal but by degrees?

—William Shakespeare, *Othello*

Practice 1

Sit quietly and recall or envision someone you know "losing it." See them as they become more and more enraged, exploding with a torrent of anger. See them carry on with abusive words, threatening gestures, perhaps throwing things or kicking furniture. See their face, how distorted and unattractive it looks. Watch this scene for a few minutes.

Now consider whether that is the way you want to act; whether that is the way you want to look. Is that the way you want to be seen by your loved ones, your children, your friends, or your colleagues? Could people ever again be fully comfortable in your presence? Is that the way you want to use your energy or are you capable of being a more creative, wise, and compassionate being? Resolve to practice patience at each opportunity so that you can live life as the wiser, more compassionate you.

Practice 2

From time to time most of us have to make the kind of phone call that will likely yield little more than frustration. You call your health insurance provider to find out why your illness or condition is not covered or why they paid so little of the doctor's bill. Why is the phone company charging you for calls to a country you didn't even know existed? Your package was supposed to be delivered between ten and two, and now, after staying home all day, it is five o'clock and you are calling to find out where it is.

Before making such calls, take a minute or two to think about how skillfully you are going to speak, and no matter how unreasonable the person on the other end may be, resolve to remain patient. There are times when we are stuck in the inequities of our system. It can be extremely annoying and even expensive, but we don't have to pay the price of a loss of dignity. When we rise above these situations our material loss can be somewhat mitigated by a sense of well-being.

Practice 3

We are more likely to lose patience when tired or hungry. Sometimes the most obvious solutions are the most effective. You will probably be more patient if you are well rested. Going to bed fifteen minutes earlier can make a big difference. Don't overbook your schedule. Eat healthy meals at sensible times.

Before you list the reasons why you can't do these things consider this scenario: Let's say you had a heart attack and the doctor said you must sleep eight hours each night, take breaks throughout the day, and eat properly. If you don't, you will surely have another heart attack within three months and that one will most likely be fatal. Would you follow the doctor's advice?

Only you can bring a sense of peace into your life.

The Art of Peaceful Living

Overcome the angry by gentleness;
overcome the meanspirited by kindness;
overcome the greedy by generosity;
overcome the deceiver by truth.

—Buddha, The Dhammapada 223

Ours is a result-oriented society—the bottom line is what matters. We are also a fast-paced lot. The faster we get to that bottom line, the better. Even the advertisement we read offering a leisurely vacation on a quiet beach tells us to hurry before all the reservations are gone. Unfortunately, rushing and the desire for immediate results don't usually ally themselves well with a sense of inner peace nor a leisurely vacation. Yet so often we believe we need to hurry, there's so much to do in so little time. I wonder if sometimes we rush around because everyone else does, or because we have become accustomed to rushing, or perhaps harried busyness makes us feel a bit more important. If people knew you had time to relax would they look down on you and assume your role in society was insignificant? Worse, would you feel that way about yourself? So much hurry, so much scurry, but where are we going? We are already here. Are we speeding past the joyful moments of our lives? When do we get to live? Wisdom is learned over time; delights arise when we are fully present in the moment. Stop. Stop rushing and be with your life. You cannot develop inner peace on the run. Rest assured that patience and productivity can enjoy a congenial relationship, even on a stringent schedule. People are often surprised by how much more they can get done proceeding patiently rather than rushing. Ask the tortoise.

Khanti is the Pali word that means "patience." It also implies resolve and endurance as well as determination and commitment. Some things simply need time. The human mind is a perfect example. For an impatient mind to mature into a patient one takes time, perhaps quite a bit of time. If for thirty years we have tended to easily become impatient it is unlikely that we will now develop a depth of patience in thirty minutes, and probably not in thirty days. That does not mean, however, that we cannot take significant steps in just thirty seconds. When our motivation is stimulated and we make the decision to seriously address our impatience and anger—that can be a monumental, life-changing moment.

Mindfulness

Any methodology for developing patience requires a multi-tiered approach. We need skills that are immediately accessible for those moments when life is intolerably inefficient, unjust, unfair, or abusive; those moments when impatience or anger quickly arise within us. Concurrently, we need an introspective practice such as meditation so that we can gain a greater understanding of our internal experiences, i.e., thoughts and feelings. This part of our practice is not so much about the actual events happening around and within us, but rather about how we relate to those events. Through this type of introspection we become more in touch with our thoughts, feelings, and sensations as they arise so that we don't react while in the throes of impatience or anger. This objective, nonjudgmental, nonattached awareness is the practice of mindfulness and it is the ground for becoming a truly patient person.

In the *Satipatthana Sutra* (The Discourse on the Establishment of Mindfulness)[1] specific instruction is offered for practicing mindfulness. One should go to a quiet place, sit down in the cross-legged (lotus) position, and gently but firmly establish mindful awareness. Specifically, "Having gone to the forest or the root of a tree or to an empty place, one sits down with their legs crossed, keeps their body erect and their mindfulness alert." One would, over time, come to see that mindfulness keeps the mind from wandering and dispels confusion. We have all experienced mindfulness in given moments. The development of mindfulness, so that we become more awake in everyday life, begins with knowing when mindfulness occurs—in other words, we must know its nature. Then we encourage more frequent mindful moments so that they occur with greater regularity.

It is significant to understand mindfulness as a *wholesome quality* (to use the Buddhist terminology) and to also understand that a wholesome and an unwholesome quality (such as

1. Majjhima Nikaya 10.

greed, hatred, or delusion) cannot exist on a conscious level in the same moment. It can appear as if they do because there can be many factors at play in the mind (motivations, intentions, and so forth) but in the exact moment of commencing an action only one intention can be at the fore. The practice of mindfulness offers us a clear and accurate reading of our "state of mind" before we act in a given situation. As taught in the Satipatthana Sutra, mindfulness meditation is developed by becoming aware of when mindfulness is present and when it is not. For the person working on developing a level of patience that is deep and easeful, this is an invaluable practice.

That doesn't mean we become perfect, saintly, or one who can walk on the waters of the Ganges, but one who remains calm and dignified in the most trying of circumstances. Impatience or anger can still arise, and undoubtedly will, but we have learned to be mindful of our feelings as they arise so we can calmly observe them rather than react to them. In that way we don't exacerbate what may already be a difficult situation. When we undertake this type of introspection, mindfulness is necessary because it is the quality that helps us maintain awareness of the specific occurrences arising in the moment. Developing true patience is therefore accomplished through quiet self-examination combined with integrative experience with others. This is the development of patience through insight, wisdom, and compassion. This is *the art of peaceful living*.

From the Buddhist perspective one might say there are no nouns, there are only verbs. All phenomena are in a constant state of change; the true condition of all things is that of *becoming*, becoming something new in each minuscule time frame. Nothing is static, nothing is permanent, nothing is as it was a moment ago. This is in accordance with the law of impermanence as put forth by the Buddha more than 2,500 years ago and today posited by the scientific community as well. If everything is changing in every moment then we need not feel locked into habitual reactive thinking or unskillful, conditioned behavior patterns. We may lose patience and act in a way that is not in accord with the person we want to be, but that is all that happened—we acted unskillfully. A moment later, in a similar situation, we might behave quite differently. The point is, we are malleable. We are also extremely complex beings. No one is simply an impatient person. We might lose our patience more often than we would like, but there are also many instances when we have remained patient when others "lost it." If you frequently act in an impatient or angry manner you will undoubtedly have regrets as you cause yourself and others considerable dukkha. It is natural that you would want to change and there is no question that you can.

We know the destructive potential of impatience and anger and we each have had our encounters with these powerful emotions. Your insights and negative experiences can provide the motivation, the juice, and the determination needed to embark upon and sustain your journey toward more peaceful living.

Now, suppose you had a close and trusted friend whom you could rely on to protect you every time a potentially contentious situation was brewing, or when delays, incompetence, or disrespect were pushing your buttons. Suppose further that your trusted friend was trained to sense such situations before they got out of hand and would whisper in your ear, "Patience." In most instances just hearing that one word *patience* would be enough to stop you from letting your burgeoning feelings escalate and keep you from fueling the aroused embers. It would slow you down, remind you to breathe, allow you the opportunity to regain your composure. Your friend would, in effect, be creating a pause between the event you were experiencing and your reaction to that event. It is in that pause that patience can arise and flourish. Therefore, I view that pause as *sacred*. It can save dignity, it can save relationships, it can even save lives. It is indeed, sacred.

You actually have such a friend—it is your mind, although it would be more accurate to say that your mind will become that trusted friend once you guide it through some basic mindfulness training. The Dhammapada, one of the most beloved of all Buddhist texts, begins, "All that we are is a result of what we have thought; it arises with our thoughts; with our thoughts we make the world." This does not mean that we are now a fixed entity brought about by our thoughts. Rather, our experience of this moment is the result of our thoughts that have preceded this moment, and that our thoughts in this moment are determining our experience of our next moments. Further, as stated in the charmingly named *Honeyball* discourse,[2] "That which one thinks about is what the mind proliferates." If we view things compassionately, the mind will create an even more compassionate view of things and thus our compassion grows. Now let's see how to put this to practical use in developing patience.

Thought precedes action. Granted, occasionally we experience actions that are so strange it is hard to believe any thought

---

2. Majjhima Nikaya 18.

preceded them. (Hopefully, such actions are not our own.) Nevertheless, even if it is but barely perceptible, thought precedes deed. Fortunately, we can train the mind and change behavior patterns no matter how deeply rooted they may be. We have dispositions, inclinations, propensities, and history, as well as a repository of powerful habit energy, but we are not hardwired in some unalterable state. The idea that we are is a popular misconception perhaps created to explain why we so often repeat certain unskillful actions. The reality is that everything changes and we can encourage the changes we feel will be beneficial, the changes that will alleviate our stress, anxiety, and suffering.

However, when faced with the kind of situation that can cause us to become impatient, the untrained mind is not likely to suddenly remember *patience.* The reason for that is we don't ordinarily bring the word to mind on a regular basis. It is not readily at the fore. Then, when a situation is becoming grossly annoying or utterly frustrating, patience is not likely to be the first thought that comes to mind. More likely our thoughts would go to our desire to alter the circumstances around us.

We can change that. We can train the mind in a way that will make the word *patience* readily available. Here is a deceptively simple yet highly effective program that can be done over a two- to four-week period. Working this exercise will help prevent the damage that can be done by a single burst of anger, and it will lay the ground for the development of true patience. Each day during the training period, think *patience* just as you are about to do a specific activity that you tend to do fairly often on most days. This is an exercise designed to repeatedly bring the word *patience* to mind. You are not likely to need patience while doing any of these daily activities. You will be training the mind in a way similar to how we train the muscles of the body. In most cases it will be best to use only one of these exercises per day:

- If you send a lot of e-mails, every time you are about to press the Send button, think, *patience.*
- If you make phone calls regularly throughout the day, just before you dial, think, *patience.*
- While reading the newspaper, as you are about to turn each page, think, *patience.*
- At meals, as you are bringing the fork to your mouth, think, *patience*;
  or each time you bring a glass to your lips, think, *patience.*
- Every time you are about to touch a handle to open a door, think, *patience.*
- Every time you are going to stand up, think, *patience.*
- Every time you are about to sit down, think, *patience.*
- Every time you change the channel on the television, think, *patience.*

These are just examples. Make up other versions of this practice in accordance with your regular activities. For instance, I often play a word game on my iPad and when I am doing the training, each time I change the words of the game, I think, *patience.* The practice itself is quite easy to do. The most challenging part is remembering to do the exercise throughout the day. If it helps, try training every other day or on alternate weeks: a week of training and a week off. The important thing is to stick with the schedule you set up; consistency reaps rewards. Just like training the body, training the mind works best when you train regularly. There may be times when the exercise itself feels annoying. To be absolutely honest, the practice is no more exhilarating than thirty minutes on a treadmill, but the results can be life-altering.

Sometimes it is wise to state the obvious. If, in a given circumstance, you become adamant that the behavior of another is so offensive or the conditions to which you are being subjected are so unacceptable that you decide to no longer be patient, then you are, in that moment, willing to undermine your progress, and understand that you must live with the consequences. My own experience is that as patience develops, those circumstances diminish. I believe your experience will be similar, especially as you see that you are the one who is hurt most by your loss of patience. No matter what the external circumstances, your impatience can only exist within you. You develop patience by working on yourself, not by attempting to change others.

At first, even with the best intentions, you might do the practice for a few minutes and then forget. What a perfect time to practice patience with yourself. Everything we endeavor to learn is most difficult in the beginning, whether it is a new language, playing the piano, or riding a bike. Just return to the practice as soon as you remember. Think of the enormous benefits of developing real patience. Be creative and let it be fun; no one looks forward to drudgery. Also, this part of the practice is not intended to be ongoing. You will soon move to deeper levels and become a master. Give it a fair trial for at least two weeks and then practice as needed. After the first few days begin to notice if there is a feeling that comes up as you think *patience*. Don't force anything, just be aware of whether the tone of the feeling is pleasant, unpleasant, or neutral. If you stay with this practice it can be very effective. If you let it go, the next time you lose your patience or find yourself agitated or angry, you can go back and train again for a week or two. The patience you are developing is both calm and vibrant. You are practicing the kind of skillful means that we can think of as compassionate action. It not only moves you forward, but guides you ever so gently, ever so magnificently upward as well. Remember these words of the Buddha: "It is easy to do things that are not good and cause harm to oneself, but what is good and beneficial can be quite difficult to do."[3]

> In a crowd or a traffic jam if I focus on one individual and develop patience for him, I can be more patient with the whole situation and all the people involved.
>
> —A chef

Insight

The next step in our multitiered approach involves developing patience through wisdom, ultimately to the point where it becomes as if it is a characteristic of who you are. You will still experience stress, delays, incompetence, thoughtlessness, selfish-

3. The Dhammapada 163.

ness, and, yes, impatience, just like everyone else; but you will be mindful of the feelings that are arising within you. You will know them and calmly be able to identify them. Most important, you will know that they are just feelings and you don't have to react to them.

In chapter 2, *Patience with Self*, we looked at a method for developing a basic meditation practice. In most Buddhist traditions one approaches the practice of meditation by first developing *samatha*, or "calm abiding." (If you want to practice meditation but don't want to be a Buddhist, don't be concerned. Sitting in meditation doesn't make you a Buddhist any more than sitting in a field makes you a cow.) It is through samatha that we develop concentration. We start with concentration because it is difficult to train the mind if it is constantly jumping from one thought to another, unable to stay with a single-pointed focus on one mental object for a reasonable length of time. We say "reasonable" because concentration capabilities vary from one individual to the next. It can also be misleading to suggest that a meditation session in which your concentration seems to be well focused is somehow "better" than a session in which your concentration isn't particularly sharp.

While it is important to develop concentration, it is not in itself the ultimate practice. Your mind may wander from thought to thought, but if you are aware of each thought as it arises and fades away, without clinging or judging, you may be learning a great deal in terms of insight. Establishing a balance that will be beneficial as you move forward can be tricky, and the guidance of a teacher, or a *kalyana mitta* (spiritual friend), who has been on the path longer than you can be of value. The teacher might suggest working on single-pointed focus in one session and then, perhaps in another, allowing the field of vision to open up to include awareness of thoughts, feelings, and sensations as they arise. It is not a science, it is an ongoing, ever-unfolding process. What matters is how we relate to what comes up in our session.

Over time, the practice of samatha can bring you to a point where you can focus your mind with gentle effort for sustained periods. Also, as the name suggests, a sense of calm inner peace may be noticed, not just during actual meditation practice, but continuing throughout the day as well. Don't be discouraged if this does not come quickly. Years of anxiety and stress create conditioned patterns that will need time to dissipate. Do persevere and you may notice at least the beginnings of change early on.

Once a basic level of concentration becomes fairly consistent you can begin to open the field of vision from focusing on a single object to mindfulness of the various mental events that arise in your sitting, be they thoughts, feelings, sensations, sights, sounds, and so forth. This is called *vipassana*, or "insight." It is often described as seeing into the nature of reality, or seeing things as they really are. It is a dynamic introspective practice that can lead to transformation, liberation, and the cessation of suffering through self-observation. This part of our meditative experience reveals most directly the relationship between practice and our "real-life" activities. In our busy daily lives there is usually a great deal going on within and around us. Vipassana practice helps us stay calmly present with what is happening in the moment.

If you observe a thought or a feeling and do not cling to it or create scenarios around it, it has a short life span and will fade away. Over time you will see this through your practice of watching countless thoughts and feelings arise and die away. It is natural order: everything that is of the nature to arise (to be born) is of the nature to fade away (to die). The reason thoughts and feelings stay with us for longer periods, be it hours, days, or decades, is that on a certain level, we cling to them, create "add-ons," write our stories, our biography; all from a single thought or feeling.

Often it can be difficult and frustrating to accept that others do not always agree with our views, and that can lead quickly to a loss of patience. As we learn about the true nature of thoughts and feelings, it becomes much easier to release those that cause stress and grief. Sharon Salzberg states it this way: "I see patience as the relinquishing of wanting to be in control, of wanting something not to be there. I remember Mahasi Sayadaw saying: 'Patience is the highest austerity. Patience is the best form of devotion.'" There is a sense of joy in relinquishing that which is burdensome, that which causes dukkha. It far surpasses the temporary high of "winning" an argument. As those kinds of "wins" add up, we can find our loneliness increasing as well.

Because some level of dukkha—physical, mental, or emotional—however subtle, is always present, the patience of sentient beings is always vulnerable. While you want to be patient with regard to the results of your practice, you don't have to indulge negative thoughts and feelings. Look at them, recognize them, and say to them, *I know you, you are a feeling. You are fear; you are doubt; you are anxiety. You have no power unless I hold on to you, and I choose to let you go.* This is what the Buddha did on the eve of his enlightenment when he said to Mara again and again, "I know you." Being recognized, Mara was deprived of its power, and defeated. You may notice that by relinquishing negative thoughts and feelings more positive ones begin to emerge and take their place. Encourage that positivity with resolve and gentle determination. Experiment and learn what works for you on a particular day. You are in charge of your mind; it is not the other way around.

Samatha and vipassana are the pillars of Buddhist meditation. Samatha is the practice that calms and focuses the mind, and vipassana is the practice in which we gain insight into how the mind became stressed and disrupted in the first place. In other words, we see the cause of dukkha. We see things as they really are. This leads to wisdom: insight into how to cease that which we do to cause our dukkha. We can then forestall the mind from again becoming stressed. Thus, the Buddhist approach is not to seek happiness, but rather to identify and uproot the causes of unhappiness. Buddhism teaches the significance of developing discerning wisdom and suggests that it is best cultivated through the practice of mindfulness. With perseverance you "change your mind" and old troublesome habit patterns lose their energy. Patience prevails.

> *The things that are out of my control are primarily the ones that can most anger me. I know I am not in charge of how someone else thinks or sees me. I am only in charge of what I think and how I see me. Once I bring this to mind patience is restored.*
>
> —A WISE FRIEND

Patience as a Way of Life

Whether or not you choose to work with the above practices, you deserve the joy and ease of peaceful living. This can be the ground of your entire life experience. Meditation is an essential practice for millions of people around the world, but it certainly is not the only path to joy and inner peace. Whatever your chosen way, it will be challenged by the constantly rising and receding tides of human experience; the vicissitudes, disruptions, and anomalies that are woven into the fabric of life along with its joys, beauty, and delights. That is just the way things are. Meditators know that life is not lived only on the cushion. We need to integrate our developing insights into our everyday activities.

There are practices that can specifically support the integration of patience into our relationships and daily endeavors. Generosity, for instance, is viewed as having a direct correlation to patience because the time we commit to our practice is considered a great gift we give ourselves and our loved ones. Generosity is seen as an antidote to greed and clinging, which cause so much of our dukkha. When aspiring students came to the Buddha he taught them about generosity first before teaching them meditation. Living a moral life begins with a heart open and responsive to the needs of others. Often, we must be particularly patient with the needs of those physically or mentally challenged. In New York City where I live, our buses have entranceways that lower so that those in wheelchairs can gain access. It takes time for the platform to lower into position and for the passenger to carefully enter the bus. As a traveler on that bus you might be behind schedule that day and experience frustration as this process slowly unfolds. With patience we have the opportunity to relate on a deeper level to the experience of others, those whose needs in a given moment may be considerably greater than our own.

When driving a car you could let someone in ahead of you. Notice how it feels to be generous and patient even at the cost of arriving at your destination a minute or two later. Not only do we enjoy greater ease, but it makes us a more welcome presence in the world.

We can reframe our approach to generosity from "All right, I know I have to make a donation, how little can I get away with giving?" to "Now I have an opportunity to be generous. I want to give as much as I can." That slight shift in thinking can be so significant. It is no longer about *me* and *my* needs. The heart and mind become spacious and less constricted. You are encouraging a generous spirit within and allowing compassion to flourish more easily. Taking time to consider and respond to the needs of others is a beautiful way to develop patience.

In Pali, *nekkhamma* means "relinquishing," or "letting go." It is a multifaceted practice that can be particularly challenging when we apply it to relinquishing opinions that we hold on to adamantly. Your budding practice of patience can be seriously tested when someone is challenging your views. You dig in and hold on no matter what evidence the other person presents. You offer the ancient indefensible argument, "I've made up my mind, don't confuse me with facts," yet, oddly enough, the disagreement continues. When we don't cling so firmly to our opinions, we can be open to the views of others. It doesn't mean we will necessarily agree, but we honor the voice, the mind, and the heart of those around us. That is usually appreciated and others might be more willing to listen openly to your views. There's no guaranteeing it will happen that way, but that is not the point. Your intention is what's important. You cannot control the results, only your actions. You honor yourself by acting with dignity and composure. You are also developing a depth of patience.

Sometimes we have been holding on to anger or bitterness related to a particular person for a very long time. We might think, *What he or she did was absolutely unforgivable.* Consider the possibility that perhaps nothing is unforgivable. If a wound is deep or fresh, that might seem like an objectionable statement, difficult to accept. For now, just consider being open to the possibility that maybe there is a way to find forgiveness even for what we have believed for so long to be unforgivable. Explore this mindfully. To forgive does not mean to condone. To forgive does not mean to forget. Sometimes to forget would be unwise, but to forgive is wise. When we offer forgiveness to another we offer freedom to ourselves, freedom from the unpleasant sensations of anger and bitterness. It will come as no surprise that often the most difficult person to forgive can be oneself. Yet with patience and gentle determination, it can be done. Here is that familiar cycle again: it can take a depth of patience to forgive, and forgiveness can help us develop a depth of patience.

Metta is a Pali word usually translated as "lovingkindness" or "loving friendliness." Sometimes it can be difficult to generate genuine feelings of lovingkindness for an individual who has repeatedly caused suffering to you or others. A slightly different view of metta would be to think of it as *goodwill.* While we may not feel especially loving or even friendly toward a particular being in a given moment, we can always strive to be a person of goodwill. I had a house in the country for several years and one time a family of snakes took up residence in the barn. They were beautiful, and each day I went to visit them, keeping a respectful distance. Then one day they weren't in their usual place, which made me nervous because they could have been anywhere. Since I knew very little about snakes I had no idea if they were poisonous. I do know that any wild animal when startled or feeling trapped can be dangerous. While I wished them no harm I wanted them to be visible or to go away. After a day or two of not seeing them I felt it was safe to return calmly to the barn. To be a person of goodwill does not mean it is necessary to practice *unwise association*. It means to think, speak, and act kindly which, at times, may require patience.

Dhammavicaya means investigation of the truth, a precise scrutiny into the nature of phenomena. Understanding the true nature of things, or seeing things as they really are, is the ground of wisdom. We can apply the factor of investigation to our thoughts and feelings as they arise in everyday circumstances. Through practice we can become intimately familiar with our emotional and mental states as they begin to arise rather than after we have reacted to them. As we investigate, we look in a precise manner at what is actually happening internally. For instance, as the initial signs of a disagreement are just emerging we become aware of our emotions and sensations. That is the actual experience, not the scenario we create to go with it. *He is such an idiot* is not part of the actual event; you have added that piece. *I'll never get what I need* or *Here we go again* are likewise the add-ons we create. There is always a real danger that we will react to our story rather than deal solely with the actual situation. With awareness we stop for a moment and ask ourselves, *What am I feeling? What is going on within me? What is really happening?* Identify the feeling. Understand that it is a feeling, nothing more. Watch the feeling with curious interest and learn about its nature.

We can practice the same way when faced with delays and perceived incompetence. Focus on how you are experiencing the event rather than getting caught up in your annoyance. You can't do anything about the heavy traffic on the highway or the long line at the supermarket, but you can learn how not to be miserable. I have a neighbor who, whenever I see her, comments about the awful weather. In the summer it is disgusting; in the winter, unbearable. One lovely spring day she advised me not to get too comfortable, it is going to rain over the weekend. The poor lady is doomed. Every day, without exception, there is going to be some kind of weather. There is no place for her to escape. So often you cannot do anything about external circumstances, but you can always do something about what is going on in your mind. This type of investigative process is dynamic and requires an open, objective approach. We examine our pleasant, unpleasant, and neutral feelings with equal interest and nonattachment to views. People who see things as they are develop wisdom and wisdom brings patience.

One of the best ways to support the development of patience is to cultivate happiness within yourself. (It may rain over the weekend but the sun is shining now, or it is raining now, but it will be sunny over the weekend. Perhaps best of all, learn to appreciate the virtues of rain.) No one is happy every minute of the day; we are ever-changing as are life's conditions, but we can develop a proclivity for happiness. We describe a person with such inclinations as one who sees the brighter side of things or who has a positive outlook. Happiness is a quality of mind that permeates one's entire being. As such, it is not related to external factors such as wealth or material objects. Material things can contribute to happiness, but there is the ever-present danger of clinging, grasping, and the relentless (even if subtle) desire for more and more, which is a surefire recipe for dukkha.

Happy people tend to be content and grateful. "People are not grateful because they are happy. People are happy because they are grateful."[4] Such people do not easily fall under the influence of greed, hatred, and delusion, which were described by the Buddha as "the three poisons." They are instead disposed toward generosity and kindness. They are not constantly chasing after the next object that can bring a few moments of pleasure. Pleasure is short-lived and ephemeral. Happiness, while always varying, is sustainable. The person who has developed a joyful outlook and a pleasant disposition has a much better chance of remaining patient in challenging circumstances.

Patience is a natural consequence of the cultivation of compassion and love, for ourselves and for all beings. When we lose patience it is because of how we experience a situation or event. It is not because of the situation or event itself. It is entirely up to us to decide what our experience will be. The Buddha taught: "In the sky there is no distinction between east and west. People create distinctions out of their own thoughts and then believe

4. Brother David Steindl-Rast.

them to be true." We create our experience and believe it to be reality. When others don't perceive things as we do we can find ourselves in conflict. We might lose patience. As wisdom develops, however, we see that there is nothing wrong, nothing to defend, there are just different views. We learn to think differently: *How can I move toward peace rather than perpetuate conflict?* Look deeply. When you really see the other person, compassion arises. A compassionate view of other beings remains essentially consistent even if they act poorly or are unkind to you.

Ultimately, the art of peaceful living comes down to living compassionately and wisely. With patience compassion arises; with patience wisdom arises; with patience we are at peace.

CONTEMPLATION

When you are inspired by a great purpose,
all thoughts break their bonds;
the mind transcends limitations,
consciousness unfolds in every direction,
and you find yourself in a new, unbounded,
and glorious world.
You realize yourself to be a greater person by far
than you ever imagined you could be.

—PATANJALI (INDIA, 250 BCE)

ACKNOWLEDGMENTS

I am deeply grateful to: My editor and friend, Sara Carder, who again has had faith in me and brought her expertise and guidance unstintingly to this venture; Joel Fotinos and all of the wonderful and talented people at Tarcher; Andrew Yackira, Sara's gracious assistant; Brianna Yamashita for her dedication to spreading the word; Loretta Barrett, my truthful and joyfully supportive agent; Nita Ybarra for creating a cover that is gorgeous and perfect; Justin Stone-Diaz for bringing me into the world of social media; Paulette Callen for her many hours of transcribing recorded material; the Community Meditation Center members who are an ongoing source of inspiration.

I am particularly grateful to the many dharma teachers who have patiently shared their abundant wisdom and profoundly influenced my life, particularly Thich Nhat Hanh, Joseph Goldstein, Stephen Batchelor, Yongey Mingyur Rinpoche, Tsoknyi Rinpoche, His Holiness the

Dalai Lama, and especially my friend and primary teacher since 2002, Sharon Salzberg. I am especially grateful to Andrew Olendzki for his scholarly guidance.

Finally, my deepest gratitude to my perfect partner, Susanna, with whom I have shared an abundance of patient and impatient moments for more than two decades. Her support, nurturing, grace, and loving-kindness is as much a part of this book as any words I have written.

The dharma offered herein is perfect in the beginning, perfect in the middle, and perfect at the end. The author, however, is a mere work in progress. Any error, inaccuracy, or unskillfulness in presenting the teachings herein is entirely my doing.

Allan Lokos
New York City, 2011

APPENDIX A

"I Feel . . ." Words

It is wise to be in touch with our feelings, especially when we sense a conversation may turn confrontational. If we take a moment to patiently connect with ourselves, then we can start our next sentence with, "I feel . . ." rather than respond in a conditioned or aggressive manner. Here is a list of words that can be useful in identifying feelings more easily. Spend time with the list so that one or more of these words might come to mind more easily when things begin to heat up.

abused
abusive
accepted
accepting
accommodating
accomplished
active
admired
adored
adversarial
affected
affectionate
aggressive
agitated
agreeable

Appendix A

alive
alone
amazed
amused
angry
anguished
annoyed
anxious
appreciated
appreciative
apprehensive
approved
arrogant
ashamed
astonished
at ease
at home
attracted
attractive
audacious
authentic
awake
bad
beautiful
belligerent
bereft
betrayed
bewildered
bitter
blessed
bored
bound
brave
bubbly
bullied
callous
calm
cautious
certain
chaotic
cheerful
clever
close
cold
comfortable
comforted
compassionate
concerned
condemned
confident
confined
conflicted
confused
considered
constricted
contempt
content
controlled
controlling
cooperative
courageous
coy
cranky
crazy
creative
critical
criticized
cross
cruel
crushed
curious
defeated
dejected
delighted
delirious
deluded
demanding
dependent
depressed
despairing
destitute
detached
determined
devalued
devastated
diminished
disappointed
discouraged
disgust
disheartened
disillusioned
dismal
dissatisfied

distant
distressed
dominated
domineering
doubtful
down
dreadful
dynamic
eager
ecstatic
embarrassed
empowered
empty
encouraged
energetic
enlightened
enraged
enthusiastic
envious
excited
exploited
exuberant
fantastic
fascinated
fatherly
fatigued
fearful
flabbergasted
foolish
forced
fortunate
frazzled
free
friendly
frustrated
fulfilled
full
furious
giddy
glad
gloomy
glorious
good
grateful
gratified
great
greedy
grouchy
guilty
happy
harsh
hated
heard
heartbroken
heavy
helpless
hesitant
hopeful
hopeless
horrified
hostile
humiliated
hurt
hyper
ignorant
impatient
important
impoverished
impulsive
in awe
incapable
independent
indifferent
indignant
indulgent
inferior
infuriated
insecure
insensitive
inspired
interested
intimidated
intolerant
intrigued
invulnerable
irate
irresponsible
irritable
irritated
isolated
jealous
joyful
joyous

judged
judgmental
kind
lazy
liberated
light
lightheaded
likable
liked
limited
lonely
lost
lousy
loved
loving
malicious
manipulated
manipulative
melancholic
mellow
miserable
misunderstood
moody
motherly
moved
needy
negative
nervous
offended
optimistic
original
outraged
overjoyed
overwhelmed
pacified
panicky
paralyzed
paranoid
passionate
passive
pathetic
patient
peaceful
perplexed
perturbed
pessimistic
petrified
pleased
poor
positive
possessive
powerful
powerless
preoccupied
pressured
procrastinating
proud
provoked
punished
puzzled
quiet
rage
realistic
reassured
receptive
regretful
rejected
relaxed
relieved
remorseful
repressed
resentful
reserved
resigned
resistant
ridiculous
rigid
ruthless
sad
sadistic
satisfied
scared
secure
self-accepting
self-condemning
self-destructive
self-hatred
selfish
self-pitying
self-sabotaging
sensitive
serene
sexy

sheepish
shocked
shy
sick
skeptical
small
sorry
special
stiff
stimulated
stressed
strong
stubborn
stupefied
superior
sure
surprised
sweet
sympathetic
temperamental
tender
tense
terrific
thankful
threatened
thrilled
timid
tired
tolerant
tormented
touched
tough
troubled
uncertain
uncomfortable
unconcerned
understanding
understood
uneasy
unhappy
unkind
unsure
upbeat
uplifted
upset
useful
useless
valued
victimized
vindictive
violent
vulnerable
warm
weak
weepy
well
well-meaning
wise
withdrawn
woeful
wonderful
worked up
worn-out
worried
worthless
worthy

APPENDIX B

Stressors That Can Lead to Impatience

Knowing the causes and conditions that are likely to lead to a loss of patience is important. When those types of conditions present themselves we want to recognize them early on so we can calmly remind ourselves to pause and practice patience. Look through the following list often and remind yourself of your likely stressors.

accidents
addictive behavior, yours and others
aggressive behavior
aging
allergies
anger
anxiety and fear
being the victim of a crime/witnessing a crime
Christmas activities
competition at work or in sports
court appearance
deadlines

driving under difficult conditions
extremes in weather
fatigue
feeling judged
feeling lack of support
feelings of insecurity
financial stress
frustration
headaches
hunger
illness
impotence
injury
insomnia
interruptions
jealousy
lack of recognition
loss of employment
loss of a loved one, friend, or pet
menopause, PMS
noise
not being heard
not having enough time
opinionated or judgmental people
overwork
physical appearance: over- or underweight
physical pain
poor communication
pregnancy
relationship issues
responsibilities; not enough help
retirement
separation and/or divorce
starting, changing, or ending school
struggles with technology
tests and grades
traffic

SUGGESTED READING

Amaravati and Cittaviveka Monasteries, the Nuns' Community. *Freeing the Heart*. Amaravati Publications, 2001. Available online. A beautiful and accessible collection of diverse teachings.

Armstrong, Karen. *Buddha*. Penguin, 2004. A short, scholarly, and readable biography for both Buddhists and non-Buddhists.

Batchelor, Stephen. *Buddhism Without Beliefs: A Contemporary Guide to Awakening*. Riverhead, 1998. A short classic, highly recommended.

Bodhi, Bhikkhu. *In the Buddha's Words: An Anthology of Discourses from the Pali Canon*. Wisdom Publications, 2005. The Buddha's teachings are vast, and this anthology is a great starting place for teachers and students.

Boorstein, Sylvia. *Happiness Is an Inside Job: Practicing for a Joyful Life.* Ballantine Books (reprint edition), 2008. Explores effort, mindfulness, and concentration with warmth and wisdom.

Brach, Tara. *Radical Acceptance: Embracing Your Life with the Heart of a Buddha.* Bantam, 2004. Poetry and kind advice from an experienced psychotherapist and Buddhist meditation teacher; deserving of its popularity.

Carter, John Ross, and Mahinda Palihawadana, translators. *The Dhammapada.* Oxford University Press, 1987. A translation with lots of detailed commentary; excellent for teachers and students.

Chah, Ajan. *Being Dharma: The Essence of the Buddha's Teachings.* Shambhala, 2001. With a foreword by Jack Kornfield. Contains many of Ajan Chah's memorable teachings in condensed form.

Chödrön, Pema. *Comfortable with Uncertainty: 108 Teachings on Cultivating Fearlessness and Compassion.* Shambhala, 2003. Tibetan wisdom for acting with an awakened heart.

———. *The Places that Scare You: A Guide to Fearlessness in Difficult Times.* Shambhala, 2001. "Difficult people are the greatest teachers," and other valuable insights.

Chödrön, Thubten. *Working with Anger.* Snow Lion Publications, 2001. Insights into anger with helpful suggestions.

The Dalai Lama. *The Dalai Lama's Book of Inner Peace: The Essential Life and Teachings.* Hampton Road Publishing, 2009. Accessible, sound advice for living a peaceful and meaningful life.

———. *Healing Anger: The Power of Patience from a Buddhist Perspective.* Snow Lion Publications, 1997. An in-depth look at anger and patience by His Holiness.

Epstein, Mark. *Going on Being: Life at the Crossroads of Buddhism and*

Psychotherapy. Wisdom Publications, 2009. A popular psychiatrist and meditation teacher candidly discusses his personal experiences.

———. *Thoughts Without a Thinker: Psychotherapy from a Buddhist Perspective*. Basic Books, 1995. An integration of Western psychology and Buddhist wisdom.

Fronsdal, Gil, translator. *The Dhammapada: A New Translation of the Buddhist Classic with Annotations*. Shambhala, 2006. The classic text rendered by a scholar/practitioner using his own stylish language.

Goldstein, Joseph. *The Experience of Insight: A Simple and Direct Guide Guide to Buddhist Meditation*. Shambhala, 1987. A classic that offers exactly what the title says.

Gunaratana, Bhante Henepola. *Mindfulness in Plain English*. Wisdom Publications, 1996. Regarded by many as one of the very best introductions to Buddhist meditation, it is a gem.

Hanh, Thich Nhat. *Anger: Wisdom for Cooling the Flames*. Riverhead, 2002. One of the more popular of the Vietnamese monk's books, it offers exercises to help release anger.

———. *Creating True Peace: Ending Violence in Yourself, Your Family, Your Community, and the World*. Free Press, 2004. Suggestions for inner peace and global change from the Nobel Peace Prize nominee.

———. *The Heart of the Buddha's Teaching*. Three Rivers Press, 1999. A gentle and fresh approach to the core teachings of the Buddha.

Hoblitzelle, Olivia Ames. *Ten Thousand Joys & Ten Thousand Sorrows: A Couple's Journey Through Alzheimer's*. Tarcher (reprint edition), 2010. A beautiful and heartbreaking account of a couple's experience with a devastating illness and how Buddhist teaching helped them cope.

Kornfield, Jack. *The Art of Forgiveness, Lovingkindness, and Peace*. Bantam (reprint edition), 2008. Spiritual wisdom from Buddhist sources and others such as Mother Teresa, Thomas Merton, the Bhagavad Gita, the Tao Te Ching, and more.

Lokos, Allan. *Pocket Peace: Effective Practices for Enlightened Living*. Tarcher, 2010. Insights and easy-to-learn exercises based on the Buddhist *Paramis*, or perfection practices.

McLeod, Ken. *Wake Up to Your Life: Discovering the Buddhist Path of Attention*. Harper One, 2002. A thorough guide for those exploring Buddhist views on their own.

Muller, Wayne. *A Life of Being, Having, and Doing Enough*. Three Rivers Press, 2011. A wise guide to the joys of contentment and moving away from the miseries of being overwhelmed.

Olendzki, Andrew. *Unlimiting Mind: The Radically Experiential Psychology of Buddhism*. Wisdom Publications, 2010. The senior scholar of the Barre Center for Buddhist Studies offers these brilliantly clear and insightful short essays.

Oliver, Joan Duncan, editor. *Commit to Sit*. Hay House, 2009. A wide range of Buddhist meditation techniques from *Tricycle* magazine.

Salzberg, Sharon. *Real Happiness: The Power of Meditation: A 28-Day Program*. Workman Publishing Company, 2010. A *New York Times* bestseller, and a perfect introduction to meditation from a highly experienced and well-loved teacher.

———. *Lovingkindness: The Revolutionary Art of Happiness*. Shambhala, 1995. This classic view of the four Heavenly Abodes is a "must-read."

Shantideva. *A Guide to the Bodhisattva's Way of Life*, translated by Stephen Batchelor. Library of Tibetan Works and Archives, 1981. A classic translation of this magnificent work.

Smith, Jean. *The Beginner's Guide to Walking the Buddha's Eightfold Path*. Three Rivers Press, 2002. A clear, direct, illuminating guide to core Buddhist teachings.

Thurman, Robert. *Inner Revolution: Life, Liberty, and the Pursuit of Real Happiness*. Riverhead, 1999. A scholar and the first American to become a Tibet Buddhist monk tells of his studies with His Holiness the Dalai Lama.

Zopa Rinpoche, Lama. *Dear Lama Zopa: Radical Solutions for Transforming Problems into Happiness*. Wisdom Publications, 2007. The author is committed to showing the relevance of traditional teachings in the modern world, and he does so with wit and compassion.

ABOUT THE AUTHOR

Allan Lokos is the guiding teacher of the Community Meditation Center in New York City and the author of *Pocket Peace: Effective Practices for Enlightened Living*. He has taught at New York Insight Meditation Center, New York Open Center, Insight Meditation Community of Washington, Columbia University Teachers College, Marymount College, and the Rubin Museum.

He has studied with such renowned teachers as Sharon Salzberg, Thich Nhat Hanh, Joseph Goldstein, Andrew Olendzki, Stephen Batchelor, Yongey Mingyur Rinpoche, and Tsoknyi Rinpoche.

Earlier in this life he was a professional singer appearing in the original Broadway productions of *Oliver!* and *Pickwick*.